Being a Writer™

Funding for Developmental Studies Center has been generously provided by:

The Annenberg Foundation, Inc.

The Atlantic Philanthropies (USA) Inc.

Booth Ferris Foundation

The Robert Bowne Foundation, Inc.

The Annie E. Casey Foundation

Center for Substance Abuse Prevention
    U.S. Department of Health and Human Services

The Danforth Foundation

The DuBarry Foundation

The Ford Foundation

Google Inc.

William T. Grant Foundation

Evelyn and Walter Haas, Jr. Fund

Walter and Elise Haas Fund

The Horace Hagedorn Foundation

J. David and Pamela Hakman Family Foundation

Hasbro Children's Foundation

Charles Hayden Foundation

The William Randolph Hearst Foundations

Clarence E. Heller Charitable Foundation

The William and Flora Hewlett Foundation

The James Irvine Foundation

The Robert Wood Johnson Foundation

Walter S. Johnson Foundation

Ewing Marion Kauffman Foundation

W.K. Kellogg Foundation

John S. and James L. Knight Foundation

Lilly Endowment, Inc.

Longview Foundation

Louis R. Lurie Foundation

The John D. and Catherine T. MacArthur Foundation

A.L. Mailman Family Foundation, Inc.

The MBK Foundation

Mr. and Mrs. Sanford N. McDonnell

Mendelson Family Fund

MetLife Foundation

Charles Stewart Mott Foundation

National Institute on Drug Abuse,
    National Institutes of Health

National Science Foundation

New York Life Foundation

Nippon Life Insurance Foundation

Karen and Christopher Payne Foundation

The Pew Charitable Trusts

The Pinkerton Foundation

The Rockefeller Foundation

Louise and Claude Rosenberg, Jr. Family Foundation

The San Francisco Foundation

Shinnyo-en Foundation

Silver Giving Foundation

The Spencer Foundation

Spunk Fund, Inc.

Stephen Bechtel Fund

W. Clement and Jessie V. Stone Foundation

Stuart Foundation

The Stupski Family Foundation

The Sulzberger Foundation, Inc.

Surdna Foundation, Inc.

John Templeton Foundation

U.S. Department of Education

The Wallace Foundation

Wells Fargo Bank

Grade 5

Being a Writer™

First edition published 2007.

Being a Writer is a trademark of Developmental Studies Center.

Developmental Studies Center wishes to thank the following authors, agents, and publishers for their permission to reprint materials included in this program. Many people went out of their way to help us secure these rights and we are very grateful for their support. Every effort has been made to trace the ownership of copyrighted material and to make full acknowledgment of its use. If errors or omissions have occurred, they will be corrected in subsequent editions, provided that notification is submitted in writing to the publisher.

Excerpts from *From Paper Airplanes to Outer Space* © 2000 by Seymour Simon from *The Meet the Author Collection* published by Richard C. Owen Publishers, Katonah, NY 10536 - www.RCOwen.com. Excerpt from *Earthquakes* by Seymour Simon copyright © 1991 by Seymour Simon. Used by permission of HarperCollins Publishers. Excerpt from *Life in the Rain Forest* by Lucy Baker copyright © 2000 by Lucy Baker. Used by permission of T&N Children's Publishing. Excerpt from *Wildfires* copyright © 1996 by Seymour Simon used by permission of HarperCollins Publishers. "Animal Experimentation Saves Lives" reprinted by permission of Teen Ink magazine and TeenInk.com. "Animal Testing: Here Is the Truth" reprinted by permission of Teen Ink magazine and TeenInk.com. "School Uniforms" reprinted by permission of Teen Ink magazine and TeenInk.com. "Television: The Most Disparaged Resource of the Information Age" reprinted by permission of Teen Ink magazine and TeenInk.com. Excerpts from "Warning: Too Much TV Is Hazardous to Your Health" by Pete Egoscue. Copyright © 2004 from www.tvturnoff.org. Reprinted with permission by the Center for Screen-Time Awareness. "Child Frightened by a Thunderstorm" from *Official Entry Blank*, University of Nebraska Press, © 1969. Reprinted by permission of Ted Kooser. "crickets," "flamingo," "fireworks," and "safety pin" from *All the Small Poems and Fourteen More* by Valerie Worth, pictures by Natalie Babbitt. Copyright © 1987, 1994 by Valerie Worth. Reprinted by permission of Farrar, Straus and Giroux, LLC. "September" copyright © 1965, 1999 by John Updike. All rights reserved. Reprinted from *A Child's Calendar* by arrangement with Holiday House, Inc. "umbrella" from *Peacock and Other Poems* by Valerie Worth, pictures by Natalie Babbitt. Copyright © 2002 by George Bahlke. Reprinted by permission of Farrar, Straus and Giroux, LLC. "The Bells" by Edgar Allen Poe appears in *Winter Poems* © 1994, selected by Barbara Rogasky published by Scholastic, Inc. "I Love the Look of Words (text)" by Maya Angelou, copyright © 1993 by Maya Angelou, from *Soul Looks Back in Wonder* by Tom Feelings. Used by permission of Dial Books for Young Readers, A Division of Penguin Young Readers Group, A Member of Penguin Group (USA) Inc., 345 Hudson Street, New York, NY 10014. All rights reserved. "Windshield Wiper" from *Chortles* by Eve Merriam. Copyright © 1962, 1964, 1973, 1976, 1989 by Eve Merriam. Used by permission of Marian Reiner.

A special thanks to Donald Murray (who passed away December 30, 2006) for the wonderful assortment of author quotations that he gathered in his book *shoptalk: learning to write* published by Boynton/Cook Publishers in 1990.

Developmental Studies Center
2000 Embarcadero, Suite 305
Oakland, CA 94606-5300
(800) 666-7270, fax: (510) 464-3670
www.devstu.org

ISBN-13: 978-1-59892-343-8
ISBN-10: 1-59892-343-9

Printed in the United States of America

3 4 5 6 7 8 9 10 MLY 16 15 14 13 12 11 10

TABLE OF CONTENTS

Expository Nonfiction

Expository Nonfiction

Genre Expository Nonfiction

During this six-week unit, the students immerse themselves in nonfiction text about topics of interest to them and then select one of those topics to research with a partner. They write, revise, and publish an informational piece about that topic to share with the class. They learn research skills such as taking notes and categorizing, and they learn to write interesting leads and transitions to connect their ideas. Partners learn to make decisions together and take responsibility for their own part of the work.

Development Across the Grades

Grade	Nonfiction Topics and Genre	Research Skills	Writing Skills and Conventions
3	• Select an **animal** to research and write about • Q&A, ABC, and other formats for nonfiction • Tables of contents, illustrations, and captions	• Pre-research writing • Generating questions • Taking notes and organizing information by subtopic	• Commas in a series • Apostrophes to show possession • Listening for periods
4	• Select a **country** to research and write about • Q&A, pattern, and other formats for nonfiction • Maps and diagrams	• Pre-research writing • Narrowing research focus • Taking notes and organizing information by subtopic	• Various uses of commas • Capitalizing languages, religions, and holidays • Listening for periods
5	• Select **any nonfiction topic** to research and write about • Explore different ways to communicate information • Sidebars and glossaries	• Pre-research writing • Narrowing research focus • Taking notes and organizing information by subtopic	• Transition words (conjunctions) • Citing resources • Listening for periods
6	• Select **any nonfiction topic** to research and write about • Explore different ways to communicate information • Introductions and indexes	• Pre-research writing • Narrowing research focus • Taking notes and organizing information by subtopic	• Transition words (conjunctions) • Citing resources • Paragraphing • First-, second-, and third-person points of view

UNIT OVERVIEW

WEEK	DAY 1	DAY 2	DAY 3	DAY 4
	Immersion and Topic Exploration			
1	**Exploring Nonfiction:** *I Wonder Why the Sun Rises* **Focus:** Nonfiction topics	**Exploring Nonfiction:** *The Seashore* **Focus:** Q&A	**Exploring Nonfiction:** *Life in the Rain Forests* **Focus:** Subtopics	**Exploring Nonfiction:** *Life in the Rain Forests* **Focus:** Problems in the world
2	**Exploring Nonfiction:** *Earthquakes* **Focus:** Nature topics	**Exploring Nonfiction:** *Wildfires* **Focus:** Natural disasters	**Exploring Nonfiction** **Focus:** Author Seymour Simon	**Exploring Nonfiction and Pair Conferring** **Focus:** Cultivating and expressing curiosity
	Topic Selection, Research, and Drafting			
3	**Selecting Topics** **Focus:** Agreeing on a topic; pre-research writing	**Selecting Topics** **Focus:** Generating questions and reviewing sources of information	**Researching and Taking Notes** **Focus:** Taking notes	**Researching and Taking Notes** **Focus:** Taking notes
4	**Researching and Taking Notes** **Focus:** Reviewing and adding to notes	**Organizing Research** **Focus:** Organizing information and researching further where necessary	**Drafting and Pair Conferring** **Focus:** Drafting	**Drafting and Pair Conferring** **Focus:** Drafting
	Revision, Proofreading, and Publication			
5	**Drafting and Pair Conferring** **Focus:** Expository text features	**Drafting and Pair Conferring** **Focus:** Expository text features	**Analyzing and Revising Drafts** **Quick-Write:** Strong opening sentences	**Group Conferring** **Focus:** Does it all make sense?
6	**Writing Final Versions** **Focus:** Transition words to connect ideas	**Writing Final Versions and Proofreading** **Focus:** Spelling and punctuation	**Writing Final Versions and Publishing** **Focus:** Author's Chair sharing	**Writing Final Versions and Publishing** **Focus:** Author's Chair sharing

GENRE: EXPOSITORY NONFICTION

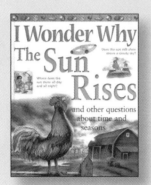

I Wonder Why the Sun Rises and Other Questions About Time and Seasons
by Brenda Walpole
(Kingfisher, 2006)

Why does the Sun rise in the morning? How did people manage before clocks? These questions and more are explored.

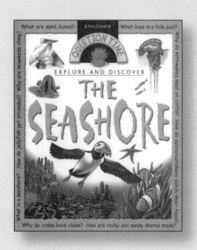

The Seashore
by Angela Wilkes
(Kingfisher, 2001)

The mysteries of the seashore are explored using a question-and-answer format.

Life in the Rain Forests
by Lucy Baker
(Two-Can Publishing, 2000)

Photographs and well-organized text offer an introduction to a fragile ecosystem.

Writing Focus

- Students hear and discuss expository nonfiction.

- Students think about different ways to organize and present information in nonfiction.

- Students begin reading and writing about topics of interest.

- Students cultivate curiosity about nonfiction topics.

Social Focus

- Students act in fair and caring ways.

- Students make decisions and solve problems respectfully.

DO AHEAD

- Prior to Day 1, decide how you will randomly assign partners to work together during the unit. See the front matter for suggestions about assigning partners randomly (see page xiii) and for considerations for pairing English Language Learners (see page xxviii).

- Consider prereading this week's read-aloud selections with your English Language Learners. Show and discuss illustrations in the books. Stop during the reading to discuss vocabulary and to check for understanding. (See ELL vocabulary listed in the lessons.)

- Prior to Day 3, collect nonfiction books, magazines, articles, and other written materials on a variety of topics, particularly topics related to Earth or social sciences (such as current events, geography, countries and cultures, natural disasters, the environment, weather, and ecosystems). Select texts that are informational (expository) in nature.

TEACHER AS WRITER

"Curiosity urges you on—the driving force."
— *John Dos Passos*

Nonfiction writers aren't necessarily experts on topics they set out to write about, but they are curious about them. They communicate what they learn about a topic in a way that makes the reader curious, too. List some topics you are curious about. Ask yourself:

- What part of the world do you wish you knew more about?

- What in the natural world have you always wanted to understand?

- What is something you take for granted that you wish you knew more about?

- What current event do you wish you knew the history of?

Day 1

Materials

- *I Wonder Why the Sun Rises*
- *Water Dance* from Unit 1
- *Can It Rain Cats and Dogs?* from Unit 1
- *Musical Instruments from A to Z* from Unit 1
- Chart paper and a marker

Exploring Nonfiction

In this lesson, the students:

- Work with a new partner
- Hear and discuss expository nonfiction
- Explore how information is organized and presented in nonfiction
- Explore and write about things that interest them

About Teaching Nonfiction Writing

There are three phases to the nonfiction unit in grade 5: Immersion and Topic Exploration; Topic Selection, Research, and Drafting; and Revision, Proofreading, and Publication. During each two-week phase, the students learn interesting ways to organize and present information while cultivating their own curiosity about many fascinating topics.

In Weeks 1 and 2, the students read nonfiction resources about various topics, particularly topics related to the Earth or the social sciences, and they write short pieces about the interesting things they learn about those topics. This process prepares them to select, in pairs, one topic of interest to research and write an informational piece about. During Weeks 3 and 4, pairs research their chosen topic and begin drafting. The last two weeks of the unit are spent exploring nonfiction craft and conventions, and integrating these as appropriate into their final drafts.

Teacher Note

The partners you assign today will stay together for the unit.

Making Meaning® Teacher

You can have the students work with their current *Making Meaning* partner or assign them a new partner for this unit.

GETTING READY TO WRITE

 Pair Students and Discuss Working Together

Randomly assign partners (see "Do Ahead" on page 357) and make sure they know each other's names. Gather the class with partners sitting together, facing you. Remind the students to bring their writing notebooks and pencils.

Explain that over the next six weeks partners will work together to explore writing nonfiction. They will hear and discuss interesting nonfiction books and write about topics that interest them.

Have partners take a couple of minutes to get to know each other. Have them talk to each other about some of the things they have written so far this year. Then signal for their attention and ask:

Q *What did you learn about the writing your partner has done this year?*

2 Introduce Nonfiction

Show the covers of *Water Dance, Can It Rain Cats and Dogs?* and *Musical Instruments from A to Z*. Remind the students that they heard these examples of nonfiction earlier in the year. Ask and briefly discuss:

Q *What do you think you know about nonfiction?*

> **Students might say:**
>
> "Nonfiction is real. It's about true things."
>
> "I agree with [Elias] because you can learn facts from nonfiction."
>
> "It's not a made-up story."
>
> "In addition to what [Wendy] said, it can be about science, like animals or planets."

◀ **Teacher Note**

If necessary, remind the students to use the discussion prompts to connect their ideas to those of others. The prompts are:

* "I agree with _____ because…"
* "I disagree with _____ because…" and
* "In addition to what _____ said, I think…"

Point out that nonfiction writers present true information on topics they are curious about. They write about these topics in a way that helps readers become interested in and curious about them as well. Explain that in the coming weeks the students will learn how to write in interesting ways on topics they are curious about.

Explain that they will spend the next couple of weeks hearing different kinds of nonfiction books to help them get ideas for their own nonfiction writing.

3 Read Parts of *I Wonder Why the Sun Rises* Aloud

Show the cover of *I Wonder Why the Sun Rises* and read the title and author's name aloud. Explain that you will read parts of the book aloud, and invite the students to think about how the author gives information in this book.

Teacher Note

To review the procedure for defining vocabulary during the read-aloud, see volume 1, page 8.

Show the table of contents and read some of the chapter headings aloud. Then read pages 4–11 (including the captions) aloud slowly and clearly, showing the illustrations and clarifying vocabulary as you read.

> **Suggested Vocabulary**
>
> **lands around the poles:** lands near the north and south poles (p. 6)
> **sow:** plant (p. 10)
>
> **ELL Vocabulary**
>
> English Language Learners may benefit from discussing additional vocabulary, including:
>
> **spins:** turns (p. 4)
> **the Earth's movement:** the way the Earth moves (p. 5)
> **seasons:** spring, summer, fall, and winter (p. 8)
> **feed on:** eat (p. 10)

As a class, select a few more questions from the "Contents" page and read those chapters aloud.

4 ▶ Discuss the Story and Generate Nonfiction Topics

Ask and briefly discuss:

Q *What did you find out about the Earth and seasons?*

Use "Think, Pair, Share" to have the students first think about and then discuss:

 Q *If you were going to write a book like this one called* I Wonder _____, *what might you write about?* [pause] *Turn to your partner.*

Teacher Note ▶
To review the procedure for "Think, Pair, Share," see volume 1, page xiv.

Students might say:

"I would write *I Wonder Who Invented Snowboarding* because that's my favorite sport."

"I would write a book called *I Wonder Why the Titanic Sank*.'"

"I would write *I Wonder What Happened to the Mummies* because I'm really interested in mummies."

Teacher Note ▶
If the students have difficulty generating ideas, stimulate their thinking by suggesting some of the ideas in the "Students might say" note; then ask, "What other ideas do you have?"

After partners have shared their thinking, have a few volunteers share their ideas with the class. Record their ideas on a sheet of chart paper entitled "I Wonder _____."

I Wonder _____

- who invented snowboarding

- why the Titanic sank

- what happened to the mummies

- what causes natural disasters

- what's in fast food

Review Nonfiction Topics in Writing Notebooks

Ask the students to open to the writing ideas section of their writing notebooks and review the nonfiction topics they have listed so far this year. Ask and briefly discuss:

Q *What nonfiction topics on your list have you written about so far this year?*

Q *Which of those topics are you still interested in writing about?*

Have the students put a star next to topics they still want to explore and write about.

Explain that during writing time today the students may add nonfiction topics to their writing ideas section, think of more ideas for "I Wonder" books, or write about anything else they choose. Make *I Wonder Why the Sun Rises* available for interested students to look at if they wish.

WRITING TIME

 Write Independently

Ask the students to return to their seats. Write the following choices on the board and have them write silently for 20–30 minutes.

- Add nonfiction topics to your writing ideas section.

- Think of other ideas for "I Wonder" books.

- Write about anything you choose.

Teacher Note

Note that on Days 1 and 2 of the unit, the students may write nonfiction or anything else they choose. On Day 3, after exposure to a couple more examples of nonfiction, they will all begin writing in this genre.

If necessary, remind the students to double-space their writing, and review that during silent writing time there should be no talking, whispering, or walking around. Join the students in writing for a few minutes; then walk around the room and observe.

Signal to let the students know when writing time is over.

SHARING AND REFLECTING

▶ **Share Writing and Reflect**

Gather the class with partners sitting together, facing you. Ask partners to briefly tell each other what they wrote about today. Encourage them to listen carefully, as they will be responsible for sharing with the class what their partner wrote about.

After a moment, signal for their attention and ask:

Q *What did your partner write about today?*

Q *What did you and your new partner do to work well together when talking and sharing your writing?*

 Note

You might provide the prompt "My partner wrote about..." to your English Language Learners to help them verbalize their answers to this question.

Day 2

Exploring Nonfiction

In this lesson, the students:

- Hear and discuss expository nonfiction
- Explore how information is organized and presented
- List questions they could ask about a nonfiction topic
- Explore and write about things that interest them
- Cultivate curiosity

About Cultivating Curiosity as a Writer

Curiosity is an important quality for students to cultivate, both as readers and budding writers of nonfiction. We want them to learn that they do not need to know everything about a topic before they start writing about it; it is enough to be curious about it and know how to go about finding information. Writing is a process of discovering that there is information that we don't know, finding out about it, and communicating about it in a way that informs and/or makes others curious, too.

To support the goal of cultivating curiosity, consider scheduling field trips to science or art museums, cultural events, or parks and other natural settings during this unit. It is also helpful to collect written resources related to these places for the students to explore back in the classroom.

GETTING READY TO WRITE

▶ Discuss Curiosity

Gather the class with partners sitting together, facing you. Review that yesterday the students began exploring nonfiction. They heard *I Wonder Why the Sun Rises* and started thinking about nonfiction topics they are curious about. Ask and briefly discuss:

Q *What topics are you curious about?*

Materials

- *The Seashore*

Note

If necessary, explain that *curious* means "interested to know more about."

Explain that writers don't have to know a lot about a topic when they begin writing about it, but they do need to be curious about it. By researching things they are curious about, they gather interesting information that they can share with others in their writing.

Explain that today you will read parts of another nonfiction book aloud. Encourage the students to think as they listen about what they are curious about.

 Read and Discuss Parts of *The Seashore*

Show the cover of *The Seashore* and read the title and the author's name aloud. Show and read the table of contents and then read pages 4–7, 12–13, and 20–21. Show the illustrations and read the captions and some of the sidebar text. Clarify vocabulary as you read.

Suggested Vocabulary

tropical: having to do with warm climates near the equator (p. 4)

sand dunes: hills made of sand (p. 5)

tides: slow in-and-out movements of the sea that happen twice every 24 hours (p. 6)

debris: bits of things that are broken down (p. 12)

ELL Vocabulary

English Language Learners may benefit from discussing additional vocabulary, including:

sheltered: protected, safe (p. 5)

stranded: left behind (p. 12)

fringed: surrounded (p. 20)

Ask and briefly discuss:

Q *What is something interesting you've learned so far about the seashore?*

Q *What are you curious about?*

Q *How does the author give us information about the seashore in this book?*

Point out that, as in *I Wonder Why the Sun Rises*, the author of *The Seashore* uses a question-and-answer format throughout the book to give information.

3 Quick-Write: Generate Questions About a Nonfiction Topic

Ask the students to review the nonfiction topics they starred yesterday in their notebooks and pick one that they have not yet written about. Have them open to the next blank page in their writing notebooks and write that topic at the top of the page. Ask them to think quietly for a moment about the following question:

Q   *If you were going to write a question-and-answer book about the topic you chose, what questions could you write about?*

Have the students take 5 minutes to jot down their own questions, and then have them discuss their topics and questions in pairs. Signal for their attention and have them write any additional questions they thought of while they were talking. Have a few volunteers share their topic and some of their questions with the class.

Explain that during writing time today the students may write more questions about the topic they chose, questions for other topics that interest them, or anything they choose. Make *The Seashore* available for interested students to look at if they wish.

ELL Note

If necessary, simplify this question by rephrasing it in the following way:

Q   *What topic do you want to know more about?*

Q   *What do you want to know about that topic? How can you write that as a question?*

WRITING TIME

4 Write Independently

Ask the students to return to their seats. Write the following choices on the board and have them write silently for 20–30 minutes.

- Write more questions about nonfiction topics.

- Write about anything you choose.

Join the students in writing for a few minutes; then walk around the room and observe.

Signal to let the students know when writing time is over.

SHARING AND REFLECTING

 Briefly Share Writing and Reflect on Curiosity

Ask partners to talk briefly about what they wrote about today. Ask them to be ready to share with the class what their partner wrote about.

After a moment, signal for attention and ask:

Q *What did your partner write about today?*

Have a few volunteers share with the class what their partner wrote.

Day 3

Exploring Nonfiction

In this lesson, the students:

- Hear, read, and discuss expository nonfiction
- Explore how information is organized and presented
- Write about what they learned and what they are curious about
- Share materials fairly
- Discuss and solve problems that arise in their work together

GETTING READY TO WRITE

1 ▶ Briefly Review Nonfiction Writing

Gather the class with partners sitting together, facing you. Review that the students heard text from two nonfiction books this week, *I Wonder Why the Sun Rises* and *The Seashore*. Point out that in both books, the authors used questions and answers to communicate information.

Explain that today the students will hear another nonfiction book. Invite them to think as they listen about how this book gives information in a way that is similar to or different from the two they heard earlier in the week.

2 ▶ Read and Discuss Parts of *Life in the Rain Forests*

Show the cover of *Life in the Rain Forests* and read the title and author's name aloud. Show and read the table of contents on page 3, and ask:

Q *What are some things we might learn about in this book?*

Materials

- *Life in the Rain Forests*
- Collected nonfiction texts about a variety of topics (see "Do Ahead" on page 357)
- *Assessment Resource Book*

Making Meaning® Teacher

Life in the Rain Forests is used in Unit 2, Week 1, of *Making Meaning* grade 5. If the students have heard the book recently, just review it briefly here and skip ahead to Step 3 of the lesson.

Explain that you will read a few of the chapters aloud. Read pages 4–7 slowly and clearly, showing the illustrations and pointing out features (such as headings, sidebars, and captions) as you read them. Show pages 8–9 and 10–11, but read only the headings, and briefly explain that these sections are about plants (pages 8–9) and animals (pages 10–11) found in the rain forest. Then continue reading pages 12–15 aloud. Clarify vocabulary as you read.

Suggested Vocabulary

fiend: dangerous person or creature (p. 12)
prey: animal that is hunted by another animal for food (p. 12)
peril: danger (p. 13)
stifling: making it hard to breath (p. 14)

ELL Vocabulary

English Language Learners may benefit from discussing additional vocabulary, including:

threat: dangerous person or thing (p. 12)

Ask and briefly discuss:

Q *What are you curious about as you listen to the reading?*

Q (Show pages 4–5 and 6–7.) *The author devotes the first two chapters to what rain forests are and where they are found. What other topics related to the rain forest does she write about?*

> ***Students might say:***
>
> "The author writes about the people who live in the rain forest."
>
> "I agree with [Laura]. She also tells about the plants and animals."
>
> "In addition to what [Emile] said, she tells about animals that are dangerous."

Show the table of contents on page 3 and point out that the author organized the information into smaller topics, or subtopics, within the larger topic of rain forests. Subtopics in the book include what grows in the rain forest (for example, "The Plant Bank" and "Feasting in the Forest"), who lives there (for example, "Forest Fiends" and "Rain Forest People"), and how the rain forest is being destroyed (for example, "Rain Forest Destruction" and "Paradise Lost"). As a class, choose one or two more chapters in the table of contents to turn to and read aloud.

Discuss Nonfiction Resources

Explain that, beginning today, all of the students will focus on reading and writing nonfiction during writing time. Tell them that later in the unit, they will select one topic to research in detail and write an informational piece about it to share with the class. To prepare, they will spend the rest of this week and next week exploring different nonfiction topics they are curious about.

Emphasize that they should not become attached to any particular topic at this point; the goal for the next week is to explore many different topics rather than any one topic in depth.

Direct the students' attention to the nonfiction books and materials you have collected. Explain that they may explore these resources as well as any others they might find (at the library, on the Internet, etc.) about topics that interest them. Explain that the students will need to share these resources over the coming weeks, and ask:

Q   *What will we need to do to share these books and materials fairly?*

Q   *If someone is reading a book you want to look at, what can you do?*

Q   *If you are reading a book someone else is interested in, what can you do to share it fairly?*

Encourage the students to try their own suggestions for sharing the materials fairly. Tell them you will check in with them at the end of the lesson to see how they did.

Explain how you will distribute the materials and have the students return to their seats.

Teacher Note

Some options for distributing the nonfiction books and materials:

- While the class is still gathered, say some of the book topics aloud and hand books to students who show interest in those topics.

- Lay materials out on a table and call groups to come and browse.

- Expand the nonfiction area of the class library and invite students to browse and help themselves.

- Place a selection of materials in several baskets and rotate the baskets among table groups over the next day or two.

WRITING TIME

 Read Nonfiction Texts

Have the students spend 15–20 minutes browsing the nonfiction materials and reading about topics they are curious about. You might have interested students visit the school library or search the Internet during this period. Be ready to assist students in thinking of different topics they are interested in and finding information about those topics.

 Write About What They Read

Call for the students' attention and have them close their books and other materials. Use "Think, Pair, Share" to have partners first think about and then discuss:

 Q *What did you find out from your reading today, and what are you curious about?* [pause] *Turn to your partner.*

After partners have shared, have several volunteers share their thinking with the class.

> ***Students might say:***
>
> "I read about tornadoes. I found out that most tornadoes in the United States happen in the Midwest. I'm curious about why there aren't tornadoes on the coasts."
>
> "I read about global warming. I found out that the ice shelves are melting near the north and south poles. I'm curious about what will happen if all the ice melts."

Ask the students to open their writing notebooks to the next blank page. Write the following tasks on the board and have the students work silently for 5–10 minutes.

- Write one or two interesting things you found out about a topic today.

- Write one or two things you are curious about.

- Add any new topics that interest you in your writing ideas section.

As the students write, walk around and observe.

ELL Note

Consider searching for nonfiction resources written in your students' native languages.

Teacher Note ▶

Note that the writing time is shortened for a few days to accommodate the reading of nonfiction texts.

CLASS ASSESSMENT NOTE

Observe the students and ask yourself:

- Are the students able to write about interesting or curious things from their reading today?

If you notice many students struggling to write, call for their attention and model writing as a class. Call on a volunteer to report what she read about, interesting things she learned, and things she is curious about, and record this where everyone can see it. (You might write, *I read about meat-eating plants today. I learned that some plants have sticky juice on their flowers. Bugs get stuck, and the plants eat them. I'm curious if there are plants that eat bigger things than bugs.*) After modeling, have the students resume writing on their own for a few more minutes.

Record your observations in the *Assessment Resource Book.*

Signal to let the students know when writing time is over. Explain that they will continue to explore nonfiction topics tomorrow.

Ask the students to return the nonfiction materials they read today so others can read them tomorrow. Remind them not to become attached to any particular book or topic at this point; they will explore many different topics before choosing one to explore in depth.

SHARING AND REFLECTING

▶ Reflect on Sharing Materials Fairly

Ask and briefly discuss:

Q *What did you do to share the books and materials fairly today?*

Q *What problems did you have with sharing the resources? What can we do tomorrow to avoid those problems?*

Students might say:

"I was waiting to look at the book about earthquakes, but the person who was reading it gave it to someone else when she was done."

"Maybe we could put a self-stick note on the front of the book with the names of the people who want to look at it."

"I agree with [Ron]. Then we can just pass the book to the next person on the list."

"In addition to what [Ron] said, I think we should try not to take too long with a book if we know other people want to see it."

Explain that you will remind the students about their proposed solutions before they browse nonfiction books again tomorrow.

Day 4

Exploring Nonfiction

In this lesson, the students:

- Hear, read, and discuss expository nonfiction
- Explore world problems as nonfiction topics
- Write about what they learned and what they are curious about
- Share materials fairly
- Assess how a solution is working and modify it if necessary

Materials

- *I Wonder Why the Sun Rises* from Day 1
- *The Seashore* from Day 2
- *Life in the Rain Forests* from Day 3
- Collected nonfiction texts

GETTING READY TO WRITE

▶ Review Subtopics Within Topics

Gather the class with partners sitting together, facing you. Show the covers of *I Wonder Why the Sun Rises* and *The Seashore* and remind the students that they heard these books earlier in the week. Review that the authors of these two books used questions and answers to organize and present the information. Show the cover of *Life in the Rain Forests* and ask:

Q *How does the author organize the information in* Life in the Rain Forests?

Remind the students that information in *Life in the Rain Forests* is organized into subtopics within the larger topic of "rain forests."

Explain that you will read three more chapters from the book today. Encourage the students to think about what they are curious about as they listen.

2 ▶ Read and Discuss Parts of *Life in the Rain Forests*

Read pages 16–23 slowly and clearly, showing the illustrations and pointing out various features as you read. Clarify vocabulary as you read.

Suggested Vocabulary

natural treasure-houses: places rich with plants and animals (p. 18)

developing countries: countries in which many people are poor and living conditions are difficult (p. 18)

reserves: deposits (p. 18)

cash-crop plantations: large farms where a few kinds of crops are grown, not to be eaten by farmers, but to be sold for money (p. 18)

conservation groups: people who work together to protect the environment (p. 22)

ELL Vocabulary

English Language Learners may benefit from discussing additional vocabulary, including:

flees: runs away (p. 18)

vegetation: plant life (p. 18)

barren: not producing crops (p. 20)

nutritious: providing food for plants or animals (p. 20)

anchored: held in place (p. 20)

cultivate: grow crops (p. 20)

preserved: protected from damage or destruction (p. 22)

3 ▶ Brainstorm Problems to Write About

Ask and briefly discuss:

Q *What were you curious about as you listened to the reading?*

Q *What are these chapters about?*

Point out that the author writes about a problem related to the rain forests in these chapters. She describes how the rain forests are being destroyed and how there are efforts being made to save them. Explain that the students can also write nonfiction that deals with problems in the world and how the problems might be solved.

Have the students use "Think, Pair, Share" to have partners first think about and then discuss:

 Q *What problems in the world could you explore and write about, and what might you want to find out about those problems?* [pause] *Turn to your partner.*

After partners have talked, have a few volunteers share their ideas with the class. As they report, record their ideas on a sheet of chart paper entitled "Problems We Can Write About."

> ***Students might say:***
>
> "We could write about pollution—different kinds of pollution— and how to clean up the environment."
>
> "We could write about prejudice. I want to find out why people are prejudiced and what we can do about it."
>
> "We can write about why so many people in the world are poor."
>
> "We can write about global warming."

Explain that during writing time, the students may look for information about problems in the world they are curious about, or they may explore other nonfiction topics that interest them. Remind them of your expectations regarding handling of collected materials and have the students return to their seats for writing time.

◀ **Teacher Note**

If the students have difficulty answering this question, suggest some ideas such as those in the "Students might say" note; then ask, "What other problems could you write about?"

WRITING TIME

▶ Read Nonfiction Texts

Have the students spend 15–20 minutes browsing the nonfiction materials and reading about topics they are curious about. Interested students might visit the school library or search the Internet. Be ready to assist students in thinking of different subjects they are interested in and finding information about those topics.

5 ▶ Write About What They Read

Call for the students' attention and have them close their books and other materials. As they did yesterday, have partners use "Think, Pair, Share" to first think about and then discuss:

 Q *What did you find out from your reading today, and what are you curious about?* [pause] *Turn to your partner.*

Ask the students to open their writing notebooks to the next blank page. Write the following tasks on the board and have the students work silently for 5–10 minutes.

- Write one or two interesting things you found out about a topic today.

- Write one or two things you are curious about.

- Add any new topics that interest you in your writing ideas section.

As the students write, walk around and observe. Signal to let the students know when writing time is over.

SHARING AND REFLECTING

6 ▶ Reflect on Writing

Ask and briefly discuss:

Q *What problems in the world did you explore today?*

Q *What are you curious about after your reading and writing?*

Q *How did you share the nonfiction materials fairly?*

Invite interested students to read aloud what they wrote in their notebooks today.

Teacher Note

Save the "Problems We Can Write About" chart to use in Week 2.

Week 2 Overview

GENRE: EXPOSITORY NONFICTION

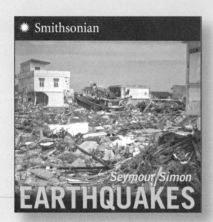

Earthquakes
by Seymour Simon
(Scholastic, 1991)

The cause and destructive power of earthquakes is described.

Wildfires
by Seymour Simon
(Harper Collins, 1996)

This book describes how wildfires both harm and help the environment.

"About Seymour Simon"
Excerpted from *From Paper Airplanes to Outer Space*
by Seymour Simon
(Richard C. Owens Publishers, 2000)
(see page 395)

Seymour Simon describes what it's like to be a nonfiction author.

Writing Focus

- Students hear and discuss expository nonfiction text.

- Students think about different ways to organize and present information in nonfiction.

- Students learn about a professional author's writing practice.

- Students read and write about topics of interest.

- Students cultivate and express curiosity about nonfiction topics.

Social Focus

- Students act in fair and caring ways.

- Students make decisions and solve problems respectfully.

- Students express interest in and appreciation for one another's writing.

DO AHEAD

- Consider prereading this week's read-aloud selections with your English Language Learners. Show and discuss illustrations in the books. Stop during the reading to discuss vocabulary and to check for understanding. (See ELL vocabulary given in each lesson.)

TEACHER AS WRITER

"Writing is like exploring…. As an explorer makes maps of the country he has explored, so a writer's works are maps of the country he has explored."
                    — Lawrence Osgood

Choose one of the topics you listed last week and write that topic at the top of a blank page in your notebook. Then write five questions you have about that topic and five places you could go to look for answers. For example:

Topic: Antarctica

- What lives there?

- Who has explored it?

- Is it changing over time?

- What interesting things have happened there?

- How is the South Pole different from the North Pole?

Places to look for answers: world atlas, library books, Internet search, globe, grandfather's memoirs when he sailed there with the Navy.

Day 1

Materials

- *Earthquakes*
- Chart paper and a marker
- Collected nonfiction texts from Week 1

Exploring Nonfiction

In this lesson, the students:

- Hear and discuss expository nonfiction
- Generate ideas for nature topics they can write about
- Write about what they learned and what they are curious about
- Share materials fairly

GETTING READY TO WRITE

1 ▶ Briefly Review Nonfiction

Gather the class with partners sitting together, facing you. Remind the students that last week they began exploring nonfiction writing, or writing that gives true information about things. Explain that they will continue to hear, read, and discuss nonfiction this week in preparation for selecting their own topic to research and write about next week.

2 ▶ Read Parts of *Earthquakes* Aloud

Show the cover of *Earthquakes* and read the title and author's name aloud. Explain that Seymour Simon is a well-known children's book author who has written many nonfiction books about the natural world. Invite the students to think as they listen about things in nature that they might want to write about.

Read pages 5–9 aloud, showing the illustrations and clarifying vocabulary as you read.

Making Meaning® Teacher

The students are introduced to *Earthquakes* in *Making Meaning* Unit 5, Week 4. If they have heard this book recently, just review it briefly here and continue the lesson at Step 3.

Suggested Vocabulary

friction: rubbing together of two objects, slowing their movement (p. 8)

ELL Vocabulary

English Language Learners may benefit from discussing additional vocabulary, including:

rare: not happening often (p. 10)

Ask and briefly discuss:

Q   *What are you curious about as you listen?*

Flip through a few more pages of the book, showing illustrations. Explain that the book tells more about the cause of earthquakes, where they happen, how they are measured, and what happened during major quakes in recorded history.

Generate Ideas for Nature Topics to Write About

Point out that the students have heard read-alouds about different nature topics, including time and seasons, the seashore, the rain forest, and earthquakes. Use "Think, Pair, Share" to have partners first think about and then discuss:

Q   *What other topics about the natural world are you curious about?* [pause] *Turn to your partner.*

After partners have talked, have a few volunteers share their ideas with the class. As they report, record their ideas on a sheet of chart paper entitled, "Nature Topics We Can Write About."

> *Students might say:*
>
> "We could write about tornadoes. I want to find out what causes them."
>
> "I want to find out more about the North Pole—what it's like there and if anything lives there."
>
> "I'm curious about volcanoes. Ever since I visited one, I've wanted to know more about them."
>
> "I want to learn about the solar system. I want to know if it's true that we can see planets from Earth without a telescope."

Explain that during writing time the students may look for information about nature topics they are curious about, or they may continue to explore any other nonfiction topics that interest them. Remind them of your expectations regarding handling of collected materials, and have the students return to their seats.

WRITING TIME

 Read Nonfiction Texts

Have the students spend 15–20 minutes browsing the nonfiction materials and reading about topics they are curious about. You might have interested students visit the school library or search the Internet during this period. Be ready to assist students in thinking of different topics they are interested in and finding information about those topics.

 Write About What They Read

Call for the students' attention and have them close their books and other materials. Use "Think, Pair, Share" to have partners first think about and then discuss:

 Q *What did you find out from your reading today, and what are you curious about?* [pause] *Turn to your partner.*

After partners have shared, have several volunteers share their thinking with the class.

Ask the students to open their writing notebooks to the next blank page. Write the following tasks on the board and have the students work silently for 5–10 minutes.

- Write one or two interesting things you found out about a topic today.

- Write one or two things you are curious about.

- Add any new topics that interest you in your writing ideas section.

As the students write, walk around and observe.

Signal to let the students know when writing time is over. Explain that they will continue to explore nonfiction topics tomorrow.

Ask the students to return the nonfiction materials they read today so others can read them tomorrow. Remind them to not become attached to any particular book or topic at this point; they will explore many different topics before choosing one to explore in depth.

SHARING AND REFLECTING

▶ Reflect on Writing

Invite interested students to read aloud what they wrote today in their notebooks. Ask and briefly discuss:

Q *What did you hear your classmates share that makes you curious?*

Q *What did you do to share the materials fairly? How did that work?*

Q *What problems, if any, are we still having with sharing materials fairly? What else can we do to avoid those problems next time?*

Teacher Note

Save the "Nature Topics We Can Write About" chart for use on Day 2.

Day 2

Materials

- *Wildfires*
- *Earthquakes* from Day 1
- "Nature Topics We Can Write About" chart from Day 1
- Collected nonfiction texts

Making Meaning® Teacher

The students are introduced to *Wildfires* in *Making Meaning* Unit 5, Week 3. If they have heard this book recently, just review it briefly here and continue the lesson at Step 3.

Exploring Nonfiction

In this lesson, the students:

- Hear, read, and discuss expository nonfiction
- Write about what they learned and what they are curious about
- Share materials fairly

GETTING READY TO WRITE

▶1 Discuss Curiosity

Gather the class with partners sitting together, facing you. Review that the students have been developing their curiosity about nonfiction topics, and that it is important for nonfiction writers to be curious about many things. Point out that learning a little bit about a topic can often lead to greater curiosity about it. Ask and briefly discuss:

Q *What topics are you curious about now that you weren't very curious about before? What has helped you become curious?*

Encourage the students to continue to develop their curiosity as they explore and read about topics that interest them. Explain that you will read from another book about the natural world today, and invite the students to think as they listen about what they are curious about.

▶2 Read and Discuss Parts of *Wildfires*

Show the cover of *Wildfires* and read the titles and author's name aloud. Remind the students that they heard *Earthquakes* by the same author yesterday.

Read pages 4–9 of *Wildfires* slowly and clearly, showing the illustrations. Clarify vocabulary as you read.

> **Suggested Vocabulary**
>
> **decreased:** lessened (p. 8)
> **increasing:** making more (p. 8)
>
> **ELL Vocabulary**
>
> English Language Learners may benefit from discussing additional vocabulary, including:
>
> **harm:** hurt, damage (p. 4)
> **necessary:** needed (p. 4)

Ask and briefly discuss:

Q   *What are you curious about as you listen?*

Flip through a few more pages of *Wildfires*, showing the illustrations. Explain that the book goes on to describe a major wildfire in Yellowstone National Park—including what caused the fire and what happened as a result.

▶ Add Ideas to Nature Topics Chart

Briefly review the "Nature Topics We Can Write About" chart and remind the students that they brainstormed these nonfiction topics yesterday. Ask and briefly discuss:

Q   *What other natural disasters, like wildfires, might you want to learn more about?*

Have a few volunteers share their ideas with the class. As they report, add their ideas to the "Nature Topics We Can Write About" chart.

Explain that during writing time, the students may continue to look for information about nature topics they are curious about, or they may explore any other nonfiction topics that interest them. Remind them of your expectations regarding handling of collected materials, and have the students return to their seats for writing time.

WRITING TIME

4 ▶ Read Nonfiction Texts

Have the students spend 15–20 minutes browsing the nonfiction materials and reading about topics they are curious about. Be ready to assist students in thinking of different subjects that interest them and finding information about those topics.

5 ▶ Write About What They Read

Call for the students' attention and have them close their books and other materials. Have partners use "Think, Pair, Share" to first think about and discuss:

 Q *What did you find out from your reading today and what are you curious about?* [pause] *Turn to your partner.*

Ask the students to open their writing notebooks to the next blank page. Write the following tasks on the board and have the students work silently for 5–10 minutes.

- Write one or two interesting things you found out about a topic today.

- Write one or two things you are curious about.

- Add any new topics that interest you to your writing ideas section.

As the students write, walk around and observe. Signal to let the students know when writing time is over.

SHARING AND REFLECTING

6 ▶ Reflect on Writing

Ask and briefly discuss:

 Q *What nature topics did you explore today?*

Q   *What problems in the world did you explore?*

Q   *What are you curious about after your reading and writing?*

Invite interested students to read aloud what they wrote in their notebooks today.

Display the "Problems We Can Write About" and "Nature Topics We Can Write About" charts for the students to refer to throughout the unit.

Day 3

Materials

- "About Seymour Simon" (see page 395)
- Collected nonfiction texts

Exploring Nonfiction

In this lesson, the students:

- Hear, read, and discuss expository nonfiction
- Learn about a professional author's writing practice
- Write about what they learned and what they are curious about
- Share materials fairly
- Ask one another questions about their writing

GETTING READY TO WRITE

▶1 Briefly Review *Earthquakes* and *Wildfires*

Gather the class with partners sitting together, facing you. Review that the students heard parts of two nonfiction books by Seymour Simon this week: *Earthquakes* and *Wildfires*. Ask and briefly discuss:

Q *After hearing parts of* Earthquakes *and* Wildfires, *what kind of person do you think Seymour Simon, the author, might be?*

Explain that today the students will learn a little about Seymour Simon from his book *From Paper Airplanes to Outer Space*, in which he describes his life as an author. Invite the students to imagine what it would be like to be a nonfiction writer as they listen.

▶2 Read and Discuss "About Seymour Simon"

Read "About Seymour Simon" aloud, slowly and clearly.

Ask and briefly discuss the following questions. Be ready to reread from the text to help the students recall what they heard. Ask:

Q *What clues did you hear that tell you that Seymour Simon is a curious person?*

Q   *How does he get information about things he is curious about?*

Q   *Would you enjoy a life as a nonfiction author? Why or why not?*

Explain that during writing time today, students may continue to explore nonfiction topics that interest them. Remind them of your expectations regarding handling of collected materials, and have them return to their seats.

WRITING TIME

3 Read Nonfiction Texts

Have the students spend 15–20 minutes browsing the nonfiction materials and reading about topics they are curious about. Be ready to assist students in finding information about topics that interest them.

4 Write About What They Read

Call for the students' attention and have them close their books and other materials. Have partners use "Think, Pair, Share" to first think about and then discuss:

Q   *What did you find out from your reading today and what are you curious about?* [pause] *Turn to your partner.*

Ask the students to open their writing notebooks to the next blank page. Write the following tasks on the board and have the students work silently for 5–10 minutes.

- Write one or two interesting things you found out about a topic today.

- Write one or two things you are curious about.

- Add any new topics that interest you in your writing ideas section.

As the students write, walk around and observe. Signal to let the students know when writing time is over.

FACILITATION TIP

During this unit, we invite you to focus on **pacing class discussions** so they are lively and focused without dragging, losing participants, or wandering off the topic. Class discussions should be long enough to allow thinking and short enough to sustain attention. Good pacing requires careful observation of the class (not just the students who are responding) and the timely use of various pacing techniques. To speed up a discussion:

- Call on just a few students to respond to each question, even if others have their hands up.

- Use "Turn to Your Partner" if many students want to speak; then call on just two or three students to share with the whole class.

To deepen or refocus a discussion:

- Restate the original question if the discussion goes off the topic.

- Ask pairs to discuss whether they agree or disagree with what a classmate has just said.

- Use wait-time before calling on anyone to respond.

SHARING AND REFLECTING

 Reflect on Writing

Invite interested students to read aloud what they wrote today in their notebooks. As the students share, discuss as a class:

Q *What can we ask [Manolo] about what he shared?*

Q *What did you hear that makes you curious about [Manolo's] topic?*

EXTENSION

Explore Other Books by Seymour Simon

Consider reading and discussing other nonfiction books by Seymour Simon, including *Lightning*, *Volcanoes*, *Oceans*, and *Destination: Space*.

Day 4

Exploring Nonfiction and Pair Conferring

Materials

- Collected nonfiction texts
- *Assessment Resource Book*

In this lesson, the students:

- Discuss topics they are curious about in pairs
- Cultivate and express curiosity
- Explore and write about nonfiction topics in pairs

GETTING READY TO WRITE

▶ Review Writing from the Past Two Weeks

Gather the class with partners sitting together, facing you. Explain that today partners will meet to confer about the nonfiction topics they have explored over the past two weeks. They will share what they wrote about various topics they explored and talk about what they learned.

Ask the students to spend a few moments quietly rereading the writing they have done in their own notebooks over the past two weeks. After sufficient time, signal for their attention and have them think to themselves about the following questions:

Q *What topics have you explored so far?*

Q *What are you curious about as you review your writing?*

▶ Discuss Expressing Curiosity in Their Partner's Work

Explain that as partners share today about the topics they have explored, it will be important for them to express curiosity about each other's topics and find out as much as they can about them.

Teacher Note

If the students have difficulty generating questions or expressing curiosity about the student's topic, model some questions and comments yourself. For example:

• "Abbie, what else did you find out about volcanoes?"

• "When you read about volcanoes, what did you find out about active volcanoes today?"

• "I'm curious about what causes volcanoes and why they are more common in some parts of the world and not others."

Teacher Note

You may want to let pairs spread out around the classroom during the conferences so partners can hear each other.

Ask a student volunteer to read aloud one piece she wrote during the past two weeks. As a class, discuss:

Q *What questions can we ask [Abbie] about her topic?*

Q *If you were going to research [Abbie's] topic, what would you want to know more about?*

After modeling some examples, ask the class to suggest some other questions or comments to express curiosity about the student's topic.

Encourage partners to ask each other questions like these and to express their curiosity as they share their writing and thinking today.

3 ▶ Confer in Pairs

Give partners ample time to share their writing from the past two weeks with each other.

When most pairs have had time to discuss their writing, call for the class's attention.

4 ▶ Reflect on Pair Conferences

Ask and discuss:

Q *What topics got you and your partner talking today? What did you talk about?*

Q *Did you feel like your partner was curious about the topics you shared? What made you feel that way?*

Q *I noticed that [some partners were doing other things while their partner was sharing with them]. Why do we want to avoid that in our community? What can we do next time to [support our partners]?*

Explain that during writing time today, partners will work together to explore nonfiction topics that both partners are interested in.

Encourage them to explore any topics or questions that came up during their conference today. Remind them of your expectations regarding handling of collected materials, and have them return to their seats.

WRITING TIME

▶ Read Nonfiction Texts in Pairs

Have partners spend 15–20 minutes browsing the nonfiction materials and reading about topics they are both curious about. Interested pairs might visit the school library or search the Internet. Assist students as needed.

▶ Write About What They Read

Call for the students' attention and have them close their books and other materials. Have partners use "Think, Pair, Share" to first think about and then discuss:

Q *What did you find out from your reading today and what are you curious about?* [pause] *Turn to your partner.*

Ask the students to open their writing notebooks to the next blank page. Write the following tasks on the board and have the students work silently for 5–10 minutes.

- Write one or two interesting things you found out about a topic today.

- Write one or two things you are curious about.

- Add any new topics that interest you to your writing ideas section.

As the students write, walk around and observe.

CLASS ASSESSMENT NOTE

Observe the students and ask yourself:

* Are the students able to write about interesting or curious things from their reading today?

If you notice students struggling to write, call for their attention and ask a few volunteers to read aloud what they have written so far. Then have the students resume writing on their own for a few more minutes.

Record your observations in the *Assessment Resource Book*.

Signal to let the students know when writing time is over.

SHARING AND REFLECTING

▶ **Reflect on Writing**

Invite interested students to read aloud what they wrote today in their notebooks. As the students share, discuss as a class:

Q *What can we ask [June] about what she shared?*

Q *What did you hear that makes you curious about [June's] topic?*

ELL Note

Next week partners will begin working on a joint nonfiction piece about a topic they agree to research. If you have beginning English speakers in your class, consider having them join an existing pair of fluent English speakers for this project. While you will need to provide support to trios to make sure pairs are integrating the third student and that they are sharing the work fairly, the benefit to ELLs of having two fluent English speakers to interact with and listen to will make this additional support worthwhile.

About Seymour Simon

excerpted from *From Paper Airplanes to Outer Space*
by Seymour Simon (Richard C. Owen Publishers, 2000)

"I began writing when I was a child. I loved reading science fiction stories, so my first story was about space monsters. I wrote it in my notebook when I was in second grade. Years later I wrote a book called *Space Monsters*. I often write about things that I remember from childhood.

"All my life I've loved to explore the world around me. At first, I explored what I found near my home. Then I learned that I could explore by reading. I read about dinosaurs, sharks, whales, and wolves and explored mountains, oceans, deserts, and volcanoes.

"With books I could explore distant places. But with my imagination I could go even further. I looked up at the night sky and learned how to find the North Star and recognize the Big Dipper. I wondered whether distant stars had planets with people living on them.

"Now I'm writing books about all these things."

"For my books about oceans, volcanoes, deserts, mountains, and the seasons, I go to the place I'm writing about and take the photographs myself. For my books about comets, meteors, the earth, the moon, the sun, and the different planets, I get the most up-to-date information from space scientists around the world. We write letters and talk on the telephone. I also use the internet to do research."

"Children often ask me, 'Will you ever run out of ideas for books?'

"I reply, 'I can't imagine that ever happening.'

"Our world and the universe are so full of wonders and marvels to observe and explore—and of course, to write about!"

Week 3 Overview

GENRE: EXPOSITORY NONFICTION

Writing Focus

- Students select a nonfiction topic to research and write about.

- Students do pre-research writing to determine what they are curious about.

- Students identify and use various sources of information.

- Students take notes in their own words.

- Students cultivate curiosity.

Social Focus

- Students make decisions and solve problems respectfully.

- Students work in a responsible way.

- Students act in fair and caring ways.

DO AHEAD

- Prior to Day 1, choose a topic from either the "Problems We Can Write About" chart or the "Nature Topics We Can Write About" chart to use to model researching and writing an informational piece (for example, tsunamis). Collect information about the topic such as books or text from websites.

- Prior to Day 2, generate three research questions about your topic (for example: What causes a tsunami? How big and fast can a tsunami be? What interesting facts are there about tsunamis?). Identify passages in your sources that give information about your questions.

- Prior to Day 2, decide if you will allow small groups of students to visit the library, media center, computer lab, or other locations in the school to research their topics during writing time. Arrange for this ahead of time with the librarian or other adults in the school.

TEACHER AS WRITER

"Get your facts first, then you can distort them as you please."
— Mark Twain

Choose another topic from the list you made and repeat the activity you did in Week 2. Write five questions you have about that topic and see if you can find answers to your questions at the library, on the Internet, or through other sources.

Day 1

Materials

- Chart paper and a marker
- *Assessment Resource Book*

Selecting Topics

In this lesson, the students:

- Discuss topics they have explored
- Select a topic to research and write about
- Do pre-research writing about their topic
- Reach agreement before making decisions
- Make fair decisions

About Supporting Partner Work

In this unit, partners work together to produce an informational piece about a topic they are both curious about. Their writing in this unit will consist primarily of factual information they have found in books and other sources. The partner work is intended to support the students by forcing discussion about the facts they are finding, what those facts mean, whether or not they want to include those facts in their written piece, and how they will write about the facts in their own words.

Both partners are responsible for the form and content of the final product, and they will decide how to share the work fairly so that each partner is responsible for researching and writing a part. During this process, partners will talk about their thinking and learn from each other as they negotiate to reach agreements and make decisions together.

The cooperative work in this unit may challenge your students. The goals are for them to learn how to handle problems as they arise and to make decisions that both partners think are fair. If you notice partners struggling to work together, use these occasions as learning opportunities. Ask questions such as:

Q *What problem are you trying to solve? Why is it important to solve it?*

Q *What is a solution you can both live with, even if it's not your first choice?*

Q *Is that solution fair to both of you? Why or why not?*

GETTING READY TO WRITE

▶ Briefly Review

Gather the class with partners sitting together, facing you. Remind them to bring their notebooks and pencils with them. Review that they have been hearing and discussing various kinds of nonfiction and exploring topics of interest to them.

Remind the students that they learned about Seymour Simon and that he, like many nonfiction authors, writes because he loves to wonder and explore. Ask and briefly discuss:

Q *What topics have you begun to explore and wonder about over the past two weeks?*

Explain that in the coming weeks, partners will work together to explore and write an informational piece on a topic they are curious about. Like Seymour Simon, they will write to satisfy their own curiosity and to help others understand and enjoy their topic. They will publish their pieces and put them in the nonfiction section of their class library.

▶ Review, Discuss, and Select Topics

Ask the students to spend a few minutes reviewing their own writing from Weeks 1 and 2. After sufficient time, signal for their attention and ask them to review with their partner the topics they have explored.

When most pairs have finished sharing, signal for their attention and explain that each pair will select one topic to research and write about in the coming weeks. Point out that it should be a topic that is new and interesting to both partners. Before they select, ask and discuss:

Q *What will you do to make sure you choose a topic that both you and your partner are truly happy with?*

Q *Why is it important that one partner doesn't just "give in" to the other?*

Q *If you want to work on a particular topic but your partner doesn't want to, what can you do?*

ELL Note

If you have decided to have ELL students join existing pairs, give the trios a few minutes to talk informally and get to know each other before they begin to work together. During the lesson, monitor trios to make sure that ELLs are being integrated into the work and are contributing to the topic selection.

Teacher Note

In this unit, pairs may decide on any topic of interest to research, as long as partners agree. This can be both motivating and challenging for young students. If their topic is very different from the topic you are modeling with, they may not benefit from your modeling to the extent they need (for example, in categorizing and ordering their notes in Week 5). If you feel that either your whole class or specific pairs will need this support, have them choose a topic off of the "Problems We Can Write About" or "Nature Topics We Can Write About" charts from Week 2, and plan to model with a topic on one of these charts as well.

Teacher Note

If you notice partners having difficulty agreeing on a topic, support them by asking them questions such as:

Q *What topics did you each research over the past two weeks that were interesting? What similar topic can the two of you research together?*

Q *Let's look at the writing ideas section in your notebooks. What topics did you both list?*

Q *It doesn't seem like either of you will get your first choice. What second or third choice might you be able to agree on?*

ELL Note

Monitor trios of students to make sure that ELLs are participating in selecting the topic for their trio to research.

Teacher Note ▶

Keep a record of the topics pairs select, and use it to help you gather resources for the students to use. Allow pairs to choose whatever topic they find interesting at this point. There will be opportunities in the coming days for you to provide guidance and help them narrow topics that are too broad.

Students might say:

"I think it's important for both partners to be happy with the topic because otherwise one partner will not be as interested as the other."

"In addition to what [Samuel] said, if your partner doesn't agree with your first choice, you might have to go with your second choice."

"My partner and I will keep talking until we find a topic we're both excited about."

Have pairs talk and decide on a topic they are very curious about. Encourage partners to keep talking until both partners agree, and discourage methods like "Rock, Paper, Scissors" to decide. You might suggest that struggling pairs spend some time looking at nonfiction books together. Some pairs may need additional time tomorrow to discuss and agree on their topic.

When most pairs are finished, call for their attention. Ask and briefly discuss:

Q *How did you and your partner make your decision? What's another way a pair decided?*

Q *What problems did you have making the decision? How did you solve those problems?*

Have pairs report their topic to you, one at a time.

3 Model Pre-research Writing About a Topic

Tell the students that you have selected a topic you are curious about to model researching and writing an informational piece. Name the topic (for example, tsunamis; see "Do Ahead" on page 397), and explain that you will model with your topic what the students will do in the coming weeks with their own topic.

Explain that today partners will do some "pre-research" writing about their topic to find out what they already know, or think they know, about it. Direct the students' attention to a blank sheet of chart paper and write the name of your topic across the top. Ask the students to watch as you think aloud about what you know, or think you know, about this topic, then write a few sentences on the chart.

Tsunamis

Tsunamis are one of the most powerful forces on earth.

They are giant waves that start out in the ocean and do an

enormous amount of damage when they hit the shore. I think

tsunamis often happen after large earthquakes.

Explain that each partner will do pre-research writing about the pairs' chosen topic in his or her own notebook, and then partners will share what they have written with each other. Encourage the students to write freely about everything they think they know about their topic.

WRITING TIME

▶ Do Pre-research Writing

Have the students spend 15–20 minutes writing what they know, or think they know, about their topic. Join the students in writing for a few minutes; then walk around the room and observe.

CLASS ASSESSMENT NOTE

Observe the students as they write, and ask yourself:

* Do the students write freely and with interest about their topic?

If you notice students having difficulty writing, ask them to tell you what they think they know about their topic. You might also ask whether they've written anything about this topic in the past two weeks. If so, have them review what they wrote. If not, ask them to write what they are curious to know.

Record your observations in the *Assessment Resource Book*.

Signal to let the students know when writing time is over.

SHARING AND REFLECTING

5 **Reflect in Pairs on Pre-research Writing**

Have partners read and discuss their pre-research writing with each other. After they have had time to share, ask and briefly discuss:

Q *What did your partner write on your topic that you didn't write?*

Use "Think, Pair, Share" to have partners first think about and then discuss:

 Q *What are some things that you and your partner are both curious about regarding this topic?* [pause] *Turn to your partner.*

After partners have shared with each other, have a few pairs share their thinking with the class. Explain that tomorrow partners will continue to discuss what they are curious about and then begin their research.

Teacher Note ▶

Collect any additional resources you can find related to your students' chosen topics. Save your charted pre-research writing to use on Day 2 and during the coming weeks.

Day 2

Selecting Topics

In this lesson, the students:

- Review and discuss pre-research writing
- Agree on questions that they want to research concerning their topic
- Identify and use various sources of information
- Cultivate curiosity
- Reach agreement before making decisions
- Make fair decisions

GETTING READY TO WRITE

▶ Discuss Pre-research Writing

Gather the class with partners sitting together, facing you. Review that partners selected a topic to research and write about together and that they did pre-research writing about the topic yesterday. Remind them that the purpose of pre-research writing is to help them see what they already know, or think they know, and what they want to find out.

Direct the students' attention to your charted pre-research writing from yesterday, and read it aloud. Think aloud about particular things you want to find out more about, based on what you wrote. Record these as questions on a sheet of chart paper.

Materials

- Your charted pre-research writing from Day 1
- Two sheets of chart paper and a marker
- Collected nonfiction texts from Weeks 1 and 2, as well as additional resources related to the students' chosen topics

◀ **Teacher Note**

For example, you might say, "I wrote a bit about how tsunamis happen after earthquakes. I'd like to know more about what causes them. I also wonder how big and fast they can be. I'd also like to research what was the most destructive tsunami ever or other interesting facts."

> ## Questions About Tsunamis
>
> - What causes a tsunami?
>
> - How big and fast can a tsunami be?
>
> - What interesting facts are there about tsunamis?

Teacher Note

In the coming three weeks, you will model researching your chosen topic, writing and organizing notes about it, and using the notes to begin writing a nonfiction piece about it. (Diagrams throughout the unit show how to model the process for the students.) The students will follow your example to research and write about their own topics. Plan to research and take notes about your topic, gathering additional resources if necessary, so you have notes to use in the modeling.

▶ Point out that you will have an easier time finding information about your topic if you have specific questions that you can research.

2 ▶ Review Pre-research Writing and Identify Research Focuses

Ask the students to individually reread their pre-research writing from yesterday; then have partners use "Think, Pair, Share" to first think about and then discuss:

Teacher Note

If you notice many pairs having difficulty reaching agreement, signal for the class's attention and discuss the problem by asking:

Q *What's challenging about trying to reach agreement?*

Q *If neither you nor your partner can agree on your first choices, what second or third choice might you be able to agree on? Turn to your partner and discuss.*

▶ **Q** *What is one question you and your partner might want to focus on when you begin researching your topic?* [pause] *Turn to your partner.*

After pairs have had time to share, signal for their attention and have several pairs report their question to the class. As they share, record their questions on a sheet of chart paper entitled "Examples of Research Questions."

Examples of Research Questions

- Why do bats hang upside down?

- What causes hurricanes?

- How did a Chihuahua evolve from a wolf?

- What is it like inside a tornado?

- Are the polar ice caps melting?

- Where does a hamburger come from?

Ask and briefly discuss:

Q   *What did you do to make sure you both agreed before making your decision?*

Q   *What problems or challenges did you have? How did you handle them?*

Explain that during writing time today, partners will agree on three more questions they might want to focus on when they start researching their topic. They will write the questions in their own notebooks and then begin looking for answers to their questions using various sources of information.

Discuss Searching for Resources

Explain that pairs may use any resources they can find to research their questions. Resources include the nonfiction books you've gathered for the class, other books or media materials available in the classroom or school library, or online resources. Ask:

Q   *Where might you and your partner go to look for information about your questions?*

Teacher Note

If you notice that a pair is discussing a very broad topic (such as "water" or "history") and having difficulty narrowing it to reasonable research questions, support them by asking them questions such as:

Q   *[Water] is a very broad topic to research. What are three things you find most interesting about it?*

Q   *What questions might you be able to write about those things?*

If necessary, guide the students by suggesting questions that are specific enough to research (for example, *Where does our drinking water come from?*) and ask them to generate a few more questions like it.

If you have decided to have small groups of students visit the library, media center, or other locations in the school to look for resources, discuss how the students will take responsibility for themselves outside the classroom. Discuss questions such as:

Q *What will you do to act in a considerate and responsible way at the [library]? Why is that important?*

WRITING TIME

4▶ Agree on Research Questions and Search for Information

Write the following tasks on the board and have the students write silently for 20–30 minutes.

- Agree on and write at least three research questions about your topic.

- Search for sources of information about your topic.

Be ready to assist pairs in writing questions and finding information about their topics.

Signal to let the students know when writing time is over.

Teacher Note ▶

If your students have access to computers but are not familiar with searching for information online, you might enlist a parent volunteer or an older student to teach small groups of students how to use a search engine. Alternatively, you might do the Extension activity on page 407 to teach the class some strategies for searching online. Encourage the students to print out information they find about their topics.

SHARING AND REFLECTING

5▶ Reflect on Taking Responsibility During an Information Search

Ask and briefly discuss:

Q *What did you and your partner do today to act responsibly as you looked for resources about your topic?*

Q *What problems did you have? What can you do tomorrow to avoid those problems? Why will it be important for you to try to avoid those problems?*

Explain that pairs will continue to research their questions tomorrow. If they have identified books or other resources about their topics, they may keep them in their desks for use tomorrow.

EXTENSION

Explore Using Effective Keywords in Internet Searches

If your students are researching their topics on the Internet, consider providing some instruction on how to use effective keywords when doing online searches. Using the topic from your model writing in this unit, discuss questions such as:

Q *I want to find out some specific information about [what causes tsunamis]. When I search the Internet using the keyword [tsunamis], I get thousands of links that may or may not have the information I want. What word can I add to [tsunamis] in my search to find information about [what causes them]?*

Write the students' suggestions on the board (for example, *tsunami causes*). Have partners talk about what specific information they want to know about their topic and together write a list of keywords they might use to search for that information. Take time after research periods to have pairs share which keywords yielded the information they were looking for and which did not.

Day 3

Materials

- Sources of information about your topic (see "Do Ahead" on page 397)
- Charted questions about your topic from Day 2
- Index cards for student note taking and rubber bands
- Collected nonfiction texts
- Chart paper and a marker
- *Assessment Resource Book*

Researching and Taking Notes

In this lesson, the students:

- Identify and use various sources of information
- Take notes in their own words
- Reach agreement before making decisions
- Share the work fairly

About Teaching Note-taking Skills

Taking notes requires summarization and organization skills, the ability to write what one has learned in one's own words, and the ability to cite sources. In this unit, the students take notes on index cards. The cards encourage them to be succinct when writing notes and help them organize their notes in preparation for writing. The students learn to include source information on each card using the author's last name and a page number (or website). Including this information will assist the students if they need to go back to the source to clarify or add information.

Be aware that writing notes in their own words can be challenging for elementary students. Look for opportunities to model this process frequently, asking the students to help you restate written information in their own words. Plan to monitor and encourage the students, but do not worry if you notice students copying from the text, as many of them will not master writing notes in their own words until they are older.

GETTING READY TO WRITE

▶1 Briefly Review

Gather the class with partners sitting together, facing you. Review that partners selected a topic to research and write an informational piece about together. They wrote down what they think they know about their topic and then agreed on at least three questions that they want to start researching on the topic.

Teacher Note

This lesson may require an extended class period.

Explain that today the students will begin doing research, both to confirm what they think they know about their topic and to answer the questions they wrote. As they research, they will take notes about things they want to include in their informational piece.

Model Researching and Taking Notes

Ask the students to watch as you model how you would like them to take notes. Use the following procedure to model:

* Reread your charted questions and pick one to research.

* Show the sources of information you found about your topic.

* Read the information in that source aloud.

* Think aloud about the information you read.

* On a sheet of chart paper, model writing a note in your own words, indicating the source in parentheses (either by author and page number or by website). Also model writing your initials in an upper corner of the chart.

Teacher Note

If possible, model using a table of contents, index, glossary, or the Internet to locate information about your topic.

JB

Tsunamis are created by giant earthquakes, landslides, or volcanoes under or near the ocean. (www.tsunami.org)

Use the same procedure to model another example of taking notes. Point out that notes are most helpful when they are brief and written in the writer's own words rather than copied exactly from the source.

Explain that the students will take their notes on index cards, one note per card. Point out that having the notes on cards will help organize them when the students get ready to write their

Teacher Note

For example, you might say, "I did an Internet search with the keyword *tsunami* and found a website called www.tsunami.org. I clicked on 'What causes a tsunami?' and I printed out the information. It says, 'Tsunamis… are usually the result of a sudden rise or fall of a section of the earth's crust under or near the ocean. [This creates] a rise or fall in the level of the ocean above. This rise or fall in sea level is the initial formation of a tsunami wave. Tsunami waves can also be created by volcanic activity and landslides occurring above or below the sea surface.' This tells me that tsunamis are created by giant earthquakes, landslides, or volcanic eruptions under or near the ocean."

informational piece. Remind them to write their initials on each card and to identify the source of the note on each card.

3 ▶ Discuss How to Share Work Fairly

Have partners reread their list of research questions from yesterday. Explain that the questions are just starting places; the students should look for and take notes about any information they find interesting about their topic.

Explain that partners will need to work together to research and take notes about their topic. Ask and briefly discuss:

 Q *What will you and your partner do to share your work fairly today? Turn to your partner.*

Teacher Note ▶

If partners have difficulty suggesting ways to share the work, offer some ideas like those in the "Students might say" note, then ask: "What else can you do to share the work?"

After partners have talked, signal for their attention and have a few pairs share their plan for working fairly with the class.

> *Students might say:*
>
> "I'm going to take one question, and my partner will take another one. We'll each look for answers to our own question, and then tell each other what we found out."
>
> "We're both going to look for information about the same question, but we'll look in different books."

Teacher Note ▶

Some pairs will still be identifying their questions and looking for resources today. This is to be expected. While you will guide the class through the research and writing process in the coming days, on any given day you are likely to have pairs working at different stages of their projects. The lesson step leading into the writing time will help you manage this workflow by having partners regularly review where they are and plan the work they will do together that day.

Encourage partners to try the things they suggested, and tell them that you will check in with them to see how they did.

WRITING TIME

4 ▶ Research Nonfiction Topics and Take Notes

Distribute index cards to the students and have them begin researching and taking notes about their topics. They may talk in soft voices during this time about their work.

As the students write, circulate and observe.

CLASS ASSESSMENT NOTE

Observe the students and ask yourself:

* Are the students researching the topics they identified?

* Are they writing notes in their own words?

* Are they writing just one note per card?

* Are they identifying the sources and writing their initials on their cards?

* Are partners sharing the work?

If necessary, stop the class to remind the students of the procedures to follow when taking their notes. If you notice partners having difficulty sharing the work, stop them and discuss questions such as:

Q *What are each of you responsible for accomplishing during this writing time?*

Q *Is the way you are sharing the work fair? Why or why not?*

Q *What can you do to make it so you are sharing the work fairly?*

Q *Why is it important that both of you do your part of the work on this project?*

Record your observations in the *Assessment Resource Book*.

Signal to let the students know when writing time is over. Remind them to write their initials on all of their cards.

SHARING AND REFLECTING

▶ Reflect on Research

Have partners review their notes together, telling each other what they learned about their topic. Then, as a class, discuss:

Q *What is one interesting fact that you and your partner found out about your topic today?*

FACILITATION TIP

Continue to focus on **pacing class discussions** so they are neither too short nor too long. Scan the whole class (not just the students who are responding) and use techniques such as the following:

- Call on just a few students to respond to each question, even if others have their hands up.

- Use "Turn to Your Partner" if many students want to speak and then call on just two or three students to share with the whole class.

- Restate the original question if the discussion goes off the topic.

- Ask pairs to discuss whether they agree or disagree with what a classmate has just said.

- Use wait-time before calling on anyone to respond.

Teacher Note

Save your charted research notes to use on Day 4.

Q   *As you listened to [Emma and Carlos] share about their topic, what did you hear that makes you curious about it?*

Point out that curiosity leads to learning and that learning often leads to more curiosity. Use "Think, Pair, Share" to have partners first think about and then discuss:

 Q   *As you researched your topic, what new things did you become curious about?* [pause] *Turn to your partner.*

Have partners take a moment to jot down a note or question in their notebooks about any new things they have become curious about related to their topic. Encourage the students to look for information about these things as they continue their research in the coming days.

▶ 6 **Reflect on Partner Work**

Ask and briefly discuss:

Q   *Do you feel that you and your partner shared the work fairly today? Why or why not?*

Q   *What do you want to do [the same/differently] tomorrow to share the work fairly?*

Explain that the students will continue to share the work fairly as they research their topics tomorrow. Provide the students with rubber bands to bind their cards. Have them put their cards in their writing folders or another secure place until tomorrow.

EXTENSION

Continue Research During Other Times of the Day

You might have the students continue researching and taking notes during other times of the day. They might use independent time, their library period, or after-school activity time. Also encourage the students to use their public library or home computers to continue their research and writing.

![Day 4]

Researching and Taking Notes

In this lesson, the students:

- Identify and use various sources of information
- Take notes in their own words
- Check for understanding
- Share the work fairly

GETTING READY TO WRITE

▶ ### Discuss Research Process

Gather the class with partners sitting together, facing you. Review that partners began researching their chosen topics yesterday. Explain that today they will continue to research and take notes about their topics and questions. Ask and briefly discuss:

Q *Was it hard or easy to find information about your questions yesterday? What made it [hard/easy]?*

Q *What did you do to locate the information you were looking for?*

Students might say:

"I looked in the table of contents of my book to see if there was a chapter on what penguins eat."

"My partner and I looked up 'tornadoes' in the index, and that told us what page to go to in the book."

"We wanted to find information about protecting the rain forests, so first we tried searching online using the phrase 'rain forests.' We got way too many links, so we tried 'protecting rain forests,' and we found more specific information."

Materials

- Collected nonfiction texts
- Sources of information about your topic
- Your charted research notes from Day 3
- Your charted pre-research writing and research questions about your topic
- Index cards and rubber bands
- Chart paper and a marker
- "Conference Notes" record sheet for each pair (BLM1)

◀ ### Teacher Note

If the students have difficulty talking about how they located information, suggest some ideas like those in the "Students might say" note; then ask partners to discuss how they might use a similar method of finding information on their own topic.

As the students share ways they located information, stop periodically to ask pairs to discuss:

 Q *How might you use [Sarah and Jason's] method for finding information? Turn to your partner.*

2 Model Researching and Taking Notes

Ask the students to watch as you model another example of researching and taking notes. Follow the procedure you used yesterday to model locating information, reading it aloud, thinking aloud about it, and writing a note about it in your own words. This time, invite the students to help you write the note.

> **Teacher Note** ▶
>
> You might say, "On the National Geographic website, I found this information: 'Before giant waves slammed into the Sri Lanka and India coastlines . . . wild and domestic animals seemed to know what was about to happen and fled to safety. . . . Wildlife experts believe animals' more acute hearing and other senses might enable them to hear or feel the Earth's vibration, tipping them off to approaching disaster long before humans realize what's going on.' What is this note telling us? How can I capture that briefly in my own words?"

JB

Animals may be able to hear or sense the vibrations of a tsunami before it happens and climb to safety.
(www.news.nationalgeographic.com)

Model another example using the same procedure.

Explain that the students will continue to research and take notes today about their questions, things they thought they knew about their topics (from their pre-research writing), and any new things they have become curious about. Encourage them to try to write their notes briefly and in their own words today.

Discuss How Partners Will Work Together

Write the following tasks on the board:

- Make sure you have at least three questions about your topic that you want to research.

- Find resources about your topic.

- Research and take notes in your own words about your questions, things you thought you knew, and new things you have become curious about.

- Share the work fairly.

Ask partners to spend a few minutes discussing what they want to accomplish today and how they will share the work in a fair way. When they are ready, have them return to their seats and begin working.

WRITING TIME

Research Nonfiction Topics and Take Notes

Distribute more cards as needed and have the students research and take notes about their topics for 20–30 minutes. As they work, circulate, observe, and offer assistance. When pairs seem to be working independently, begin conferring with one pair at a time.

TEACHER CONFERENCE NOTE

Today begin conferring with pairs to see how they are doing with researching and taking notes. Ask partners to read some of their pre-research writing to you and to tell you what they are finding out about their questions. Focus your conversations on what the partners are curious about, what they are learning, and how they are capturing what they are learning in their notes. Ask questions such as:

Q *What questions about your topic are you researching? What made you curious about those things?*

continues

TEACHER CONFERENCE NOTE *continued*

Q *What did you find out about your topic? Read me one of your notes.*

Q *What else do you want to know? Where will you go to try to find out about that?*

Document your observations for each pair using the "Conference Notes" record sheet (BLM1). Use the "Conference Notes" record sheets for conferences throughout this unit.

Signal to let the students know when writing time is over. Remind them to write their initials on each of their cards.

SHARING AND REFLECTING

 Reflect on Researching and Taking Notes

Have partners review their notes together to make sure that what they have written makes sense. Explain that if they find a note confusing, they should work together to decide what is confusing about it and how to make it more understandable. Explain that partners may need to refer to the source of the note to help them rewrite it.

After several minutes, briefly discuss:

Q *Who has an example of a confusing note? What did you do to make the note more understandable?*

Q *What have you learned about taking notes? What suggestions do you have to help others?*

Q *What did you and your partner do to share the work fairly today?*

Teacher Note

Save your charted research notes to use in Week 4.

Explain that partners will continue to research their topics next week. Have them bind their index cards with a rubber band and place them in their writing folders or another secure place until then.

GENRE: EXPOSITORY NONFICTION

Writing Focus

- Students use various sources of information to research a topic.

- Students modify and expand their thinking based on research.

- Students take notes in their own words.

- Students organize their notes in preparation for writing.

- Students draft nonfiction informational pieces.

- Students confer with one another and the teacher.

Social Focus

- Students make decisions and solve problems respectfully.

- Students act in fair and caring ways.

- Students work in a responsible way.

DO AHEAD

- Prior to Day 2, research any unanswered questions about your topic on your research questions chart. Take notes so you have at least eight to ten notes altogether. Think about how you might categorize your notes. (See Day 2, Step 2, pages 421–423, for an example.)

- Prior to Day 3, review your categorized notes (from Day 2) and your pre-research writing and think ahead about how you might begin drafting an informational piece about your topic. (See Day 3, Step 2, pages 427–428, for an example.)

- Prior to Day 4, review the informational piece you modeled writing on Day 3, and think ahead about how you will model adding to the piece. (See Day 4, Step 1, pages 432–433.)

TEACHER AS WRITER

"We write about what we don't know about what we know."
— *Grace Paley*

Reread the questions you wrote concerning a nonfiction topic in "Teacher as Writer" over the past two weeks. Choose one or two questions and try to find some information about those questions using any resources you have on hand. As you look for information, ask yourself:

- Is it hard or easy to locate information about my questions? Would modifying my questions make it easier? How?

- What tools or methods am I using to locate the information (for example, tables of contents, indexes, glossaries, search engines)? What skills do I need to use these tools successfully?

Day 1

Materials

- Collected nonfiction texts from Weeks 1–3
- Sources of information about your topic from Week 3
- Your research notes from Week 3
- Your charted pre-research writing and research questions
- Index cards and rubber bands

Researching and Taking Notes

In this lesson, the students:

- Modify and expand their thinking based on research
- Use various sources of information to research a topic
- Take notes in their own words
- Check each other's notes for understanding
- Share the work fairly

GETTING READY TO WRITE

 Review Pre-research Writing and Notes

Gather the class with partners sitting together, facing you. Review that partners began researching their chosen topics last week. Ask the students to quietly reread their pre-research writing and their notes; then signal for their attention and ask:

Q *After starting your research, did you change your mind about anything you wrote in your pre-research writing? If so, tell us about it.*

Use "Think, Pair, Share" to have partners first think about and then discuss:

 Q *What is something new that both you and your partner have learned about your topic?* [pause] *Turn to your partner.*

After partners have discussed the question, have a few pairs share with the class. Remind the class that the purpose of their research (and the writing they will do later in the week) is to satisfy their own curiosity about their topic and also to help others become curious about it.

Explain that today partners will continue to research and take notes about their questions, things they thought they knew about their topics (from their pre-research writing), and any new things they have become curious about.

Teacher Note

If necessary, model researching and taking notes about your topic again using the procedure you used in Week 3, Day 4, Step 2. Model locating specific information using a table of contents, index, glossary, etc. Read information from your source aloud, and ask the students to help you write notes that are brief and written in your own words.

▶

Discuss How Partners Will Work Together

Write the following tasks on the board and have partners work on them for 20–30 minutes.

- Make sure you have at least three questions about your topic that you want to research.

- Find resources for your topic.

- Research and take notes in your own words about your questions, things you thought you knew, and new things you have become curious about.

- Share the work fairly.

Ask partners to spend a few minutes discussing what they want to accomplish today and how they will share the work in a fair way. When they are ready, have them return to their seats and begin working.

WRITING TIME

Research Nonfiction Topics and Take Notes

Distribute more index cards to the students as needed, and have them research and take notes about their topics. As they work, circulate, observe, and offer assistance. When pairs seem to be working independently, confer with one pair at a time.

TEACHER CONFERENCE NOTE

As you did in Week 3, continue to confer with pairs by asking partners to read some of their pre-research writing to you and to tell you what they are finding out about their questions. Focus your conversations on what the partners are curious about, what they are learning, and how they are capturing what they are learning in their notes. Ask questions such as:

Q *What questions are you researching about your topic? What made you curious about those things?*

continues

TEACHER CONFERENCE NOTE *continued*

Q *What did you find out about your topic? Read me one of your notes.*

Q *What else do you want to know? Where will you go to try to find out about that?*

Document your observations for each pair using the "Conference Notes" record sheet (BLM1).

Signal to let the students know when writing time is over.

SHARING AND REFLECTING

4 ▶ **Reflect on Researching and Taking Notes**

Have partners review their notes together. Ask:

Q *What was it like to take notes in your own words today? Read us one of your notes.*

Q *What is one interesting fact you and your partner learned about your topic today?*

Q *Take a look at your pre-research writing. What have you learned about your topic that confirms what you thought you knew? What have you learned that's different from what you thought you knew?*

Teacher Note ▶

If necessary, restate the first part of this question to say, "What have you learned that tells you that what you thought about your topic was correct?"

Explain that partners will begin organizing their notes tomorrow in preparation for writing their informational piece. They will have time to continue researching their topic as well.

Provide rubber bands as needed and have partners bind their cards and put them in their writing folders or another secure place until tomorrow.

Day 2

Organizing Research

In this lesson, the students:

- Modify and expand their thinking based on research
- Organize notes in preparation for writing
- Reach agreement before making decisions
- Agree and disagree in a caring way
- Share the work fairly

GETTING READY TO WRITE

▶ Briefly Review

Gather the class in a circle with partners sitting together. Review that they have been researching and taking notes about their chosen topics. Explain that in order to write about what they have learned in a clear and interesting way, they will need to organize their notes so they are complete and make sense. Explain that today you will show them how to organize their notes. They will then organize their own notes to see where they need more information so they can get ready to write.

▶ Model Organizing Notes

Ask the students to watch as you model organizing your notes by subtopics. Read your notes aloud as you spread them out on the floor. Explain that some of the notes can be put together because they are about the same subtopic. Model putting similar notes together and naming the categories (see the Teacher Note).

Ask:

Q *What other notes can we put ▶ together? What could we call this group of notes?*

Materials

- Your research notes (see "Do Ahead" on page 417)
- Pad of self-stick notes for each pair
- Paper clips for each pair
- Collected nonfiction texts
- *Assessment Resource Book*

Teacher Note

You might say, "I can combine *Tsunamis are created by giant earthquakes, landslides, or volcanoes under or near the ocean* and *Huge amounts of water move quickly and cause giant ripples* because they are both about what causes tsunamis. I can call this group 'Causes of Tsunamis.'"

If possible, use the students' suggestions to categorize the notes, and use self-stick notes to label each group. If the students have difficulty categorizing the notes, continue to model while thinking aloud.

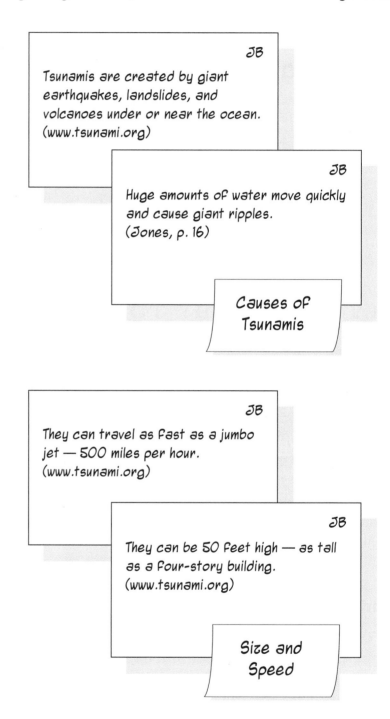

> *JB*
>
> Animals may be able to hear or sense the vibrations of a tsunami before it happens and climb to safety.
> (www.news.nationalgeographic.com)

Other Interesting Facts

After categorizing your notes, point out that these are the facts that you will include in your written piece about your topic. Ask:

Q *Do you think I have enough information for my written piece? Why or why not?*

Q *Which category do you think might need more information? Why?*

Q *What additional categories might I want to include in my written piece? Why?*

Students might say:

"You only have one fact in the 'Other Interesting Facts' group. You might want to add a few more to that category."

"Maybe you can include information about the tsunamis that hit in the Indian Ocean."

Use paper clips to attach each group of notes together with its heading.

Discuss How Partners Will Work Together

Write the following tasks on the board:

- Organize your notes into groups.

- Name the groups using self-stick notes.

- Decide where you need more information and continue researching.

- Clip the groups of notes together with your headings.

FACILITATION TIP

Continue to focus on **pacing class discussions** by scanning the class and using techniques such as the following:

- Call on just a few students to respond to each question.

- Use "Turn to Your Partner" if many students want to speak, then call on just two or three students to share with the whole class.

- Restate the original question if the discussion goes off the topic.

- Ask pairs to discuss whether they agree or disagree with what a classmate has just said.

- Use wait-time before calling on anyone to respond.

◀ **Teacher Note**

Prior to Day 3, use the students' suggestions to research and write additional notes (in additional categories, if necessary).

Point out that there are usually multiple ways that notes can be organized, and that partners will need to talk until they agree on the best way to organize their notes. Ask and briefly discuss:

Q   *If you and your partner disagree at first about how to organize your notes, what will you do?*

Q   *Why is it important to disagree in a caring way?*

Point out that disagreements are natural in any learning situation and that people can disagree while maintaining respect for one another. Encourage partners to be aware of how they are disagreeing with each other and tell them that you will check in with them at the end of the lesson.

Have partners spend a few minutes discussing what they will do and how they will share the work in a fair way. When they are ready, have them return to their seats and begin working.

WRITING TIME

4▶ Organize Notes for Writing

Have partners work together for 20–30 minutes to categorize their notes and continue researching their topics. When pairs have finished organizing their notes, have them signal you so you can review their work.

CLASS ASSESSMENT NOTE

Observe partners working together and ask yourself:

- Do partners seem able to categorize their notes in ways that make sense?

- Do they categorize all their notes?

- Are they able to agree on how to categorize their notes?

- If they don't agree at first, do they keep talking until they reach agreement?

continues

CLASS ASSESSMENT NOTE *continued*

Support struggling pairs by asking them questions such as:

Q *What notes seem to belong together? Why do you think so?*

Q *What could you call this group of notes?*

Q *What other notes could go into this group? Why do you think so?*

If necessary, suggest some categories for partners to consider to get them started. Be aware that categorizing information can be challenging for young students and that some of their difficulty may be normal for their developmental level. They may have difficulty defining categories or consistently sorting all their notes into those categories. They may want to discard notes that don't fit, or become preoccupied with having the same number of notes in each category. Encourage them to try their best to organize all their notes in a way that makes sense (perhaps creating an "Other Interesting Facts" category for outliers).

Record your observations in the *Assessment Resource Book*.

Signal to let the students know when writing time is over.

SHARING AND REFLECTING

▶ **Reflect on Partner Work**

Ask:

Q *How did you group your notes today? What were some of your categories?*

Q *In which categories did you and your partner decide you needed more information? What made you decide that?*

Q *Did you and your partner disagree about anything when you were organizing your notes? If so, what? What did you do to disagree in a caring way? How did you reach agreement?*

Teacher Note

Decide if your students need another day or two to organize their notes and finish their research before moving into the drafting phase. If so, plan time for them to do this work before moving on to Day 3.

Explain that tomorrow partners will finish organizing their notes, if necessary, and begin writing their informational pieces. Pairs who still need time to finish researching and taking notes will have time to do so.

Have partners put their work away in a secure place until tomorrow.

EXTENSION

Discuss Nonfiction Across the School Day

Take time at the end of independent reading periods and other times during the day to discuss the nonfiction students are reading. Have students share the title and author of the book they are reading and explain what the book is about. Discuss questions such as:

Q *How do you know that the book you are reading is nonfiction?*

Q *What true information are you learning about from the book?*

Day 3

Drafting and Pair Conferring

In this lesson, the students:

- Order their grouped notes in preparation for writing
- Decide how they will fairly share the writing
- Begin drafting their informational piece
- Check for understanding
- Reach agreement before making decisions
- Share the work fairly

Materials

- Your grouped research notes from Day 2 (see "Do Ahead" on page 417)
- Loose, lined paper for writing drafts
- A folder for each pair
- Chart paper and a marker
- *Assessment Resource Book*

GETTING READY TO WRITE

▶ Briefly Review

Gather the class in a circle, with partners sitting together. Review that they have grouped their research notes into subtopics in preparation for writing. Explain that today partners will put their grouped notes in the order in which they want to write about them, and then begin writing a draft of their piece. Ask and briefly discuss:

Q *What have you found out about your topic that you think other people will be excited or curious to learn about? Turn to your partner.*

After partners have talked, signal for their attention and explain that you will model ordering your grouped notes and beginning to write a draft.

▶ Model Ordering Your Notes and Beginning a Draft

Ask the students to watch as you spread your clipped groups of notes out on the floor. Think aloud about the order in which you want to write about each category, and then stack the groups in that order.

Teacher Note

You might say, "I think I will write about the 'Size and Speed' of tsunamis first, because I think those facts will really capture my reader's attention. Then I will write about the 'Causes of Tsunamis,' and then follow that with 'Other Interesting Facts.'"

Teacher Note ▶

You might say, "Maybe I can start by writing, *It's hard to believe, but a tsunami can be 50 feet high.*"

Unclip your first group of notes and spread them out on the floor. Reread them and think aloud about how you might want to start writing this section of your piece. Model writing a few sentences about this subtopic, double-spaced, on a sheet of chart paper. Point out the notes you are using as you write. Ask:

Q *What is another sentence I can write regarding [the size and speed of tsunamis]?*

Q *What shall I tell about next? What sentence can I write to tell about that?*

> *Size and Speed of Tsunamis*
>
> It's hard to believe, but a tsunami can be 50 feet high.
>
> That's as tall as a four-story building! It can travel across
>
> the ocean as fast as a jumbo jet, at about 500 miles per
>
> hour. It's hard to see a tsunami traveling across the ocean.
>
> It doesn't become visible until it gets close to shore. By then,
>
> it's too late!

Use the students' suggestions to write a few more sentences. If the students have difficulty suggesting sentences, model writing a few more yourself. Point out that you are trying to write in a way that makes the topic as interesting as possible for your readers.

▶ **3** **Discuss How Partners Will Work Together**

Explain that partners will work together today to order their notes and begin writing. Tell them that you expect both partners to participate in the writing, so they will need to decide who will write what part. They will put their parts together into one piece when they publish it for the class.

Write the following tasks on the board and have partners work on them for 20–30 minutes.

- Arrange your grouped notes in the order in which you will write about them.

- Reread your notes and make sure the order makes sense.

- Decide how you will share the writing fairly.

- Begin writing a draft of your informational piece, double-spaced, on loose, lined paper.

Ask partners to spend a few minutes discussing what they want to accomplish today and how they will share the work in a fair way. After a moment, signal for attention. Ask and briefly discuss:

Q *What part of your pair work are you responsible for today?*

Have partners return to their seats and begin working.

ELL Note

Monitor trios of students to make sure that ELLs are participating in the work. Very limited English speakers may not be able to help with the writing. If this is the case, help them contribute to their trio's work in other ways, such as reading the research notes aloud, and drawing and labeling diagrams to accompany the final piece.

WRITING TIME

▶ Begin Drafting Informational Pieces

Have partners work together for 20–30 minutes to order their notes and draft their informational pieces. As the students work, circulate and observe.

CLASS ASSESSMENT NOTE

Observe partners working and ask yourself:

- Do partners seem able to decide on an order of subtopics for their piece? Does the order make sense?

- Are both partners writing sections of their draft?

continues

CLASS ASSESSMENT NOTE *continued*

- Are they able to use their notes to write coherently about their topic?

- Are they double-spacing their drafts?

Support struggling pairs by asking them questions such as:

Q *What do you want to write about first to capture your reader's attention?*

Q *What do you want to write about next?*

Q *What part is each partner working on? Is that a fair way to share the work? Why or why not? [What will you do differently to share the work fairly?]*

Record your observations in the *Assessment Resource Book*.

Signal to let the students know when writing time is over.

SHARING AND REFLECTING

 Confer in Pairs About Drafts

Have partners read their writing from today to each other and check to make sure they each understand what the other has written. After a few moments, signal for their attention and ask:

Q *Do all of your partner's notes make sense to you? If not, what can you ask your partner to help you understand?*

Q *If your partner is confused about something you wrote, how can you revise it to make it clearer?*

Invite volunteers to share examples from their own writing as they answer these questions.

→ Reflect on Partner Work

Ask and briefly discuss:

Q *What did you do to work responsibly on your own part of the work today? How did that help your pair work?*

Q *What did you and your partner do to reach agreement about how to write your informational piece? If you didn't agree at first, what did you do to reach agreement?*

Distribute a folder to each pair and have partners write their names on it. Explain that pairs will keep all of their papers related to their informational pieces in this joint folder. Have the students decide who will keep the folder until tomorrow.

Teacher Note

Save the model draft of your informational piece to use on Day 4.

Day 4

Materials

- Your grouped research notes from Day 3
- Model draft of your informational piece from Day 3
- Loose, lined paper for writing drafts
- Chart paper and a marker

Drafting and Pair Conferring

In this lesson, the students:

- Draft their informational piece
- Check for understanding
- Work responsibly in pairs
- Share the work fairly

GETTING READY TO WRITE

 Model Adding to Your Draft

Gather the class in a circle with partners sitting together. Review that they began writing drafts of their informational pieces yesterday. Explain that they will continue to work on their drafts today.

Using the procedure from yesterday (see Day 3, Step 2, pages 427–428), model adding to your informational piece by spreading a group of notes out on the floor, rereading them, thinking aloud about what you might write, and writing.

Elicit the students' help in coming up with more sentences. Ask questions such as:

Q (Point to a note.) *I want to include this information about [how animals seem to sense a tsunami before it happens]. What sentence could I write to get this information across in an interesting way?*

Other Interesting Facts

   Strangely, many animals seem able to escape the

disaster of tsunamis. Scientists believe that animals may

use their excellent hearing or a "sixth sense" to detect an

oncoming tsunami. When they sense one coming, they quickly

climb to higher ground.

If the students have difficulty suggesting sentences, continue thinking aloud and writing a few more yourself. Point out that you are trying to write in a way that makes the topic as interesting as possible for your readers.

Encourage the students to continue to think about how to make their topic interesting to their readers as they write today.

▶ Discuss How Partners Will Work Together

Remind the students that you expect both partners to participate in the writing. They will each write different sections, and then they will put their sections together into one piece when they publish it for the class.

Ask partners to spend a few minutes reviewing what they have written so far and deciding what they will write today. When they are ready, have them return to their seats and begin working.

WRITING TIME

3 ▶ Draft Informational Pieces

Have partners work together for 20–30 minutes to draft their informational pieces. As they work, circulate, observe, and offer assistance. When pairs seem to be working independently, confer with one pair at a time.

> ### TEACHER CONFERENCE NOTE
>
> Continue to confer with pairs about their drafts. Ask partners to read their drafts aloud and to tell you their plan for their piece. Ask questions such as:
>
> **Q** *What did you write in your pre-research writing that you want to include in your draft?*
>
> **Q** *What questions did you originally write that you will answer in your draft?*
>
> **Q** *How did you categorize and order your notes? What made you decide to organize them that way?*
>
> **Q** *What will the rest of your piece look like?*
>
> **Q** *How are you going to share the writing fairly?*
>
> Document your observations for each pair using the "Conference Notes" record sheet (BLM1).

Signal to let the students know when writing time is over.

SHARING AND REFLECTING

4 ▶ Confer in Pairs About Drafts

As you did yesterday, have partners read their writing from today to each other and check to make sure they each understand what the other has written. After a few moments, signal for their attention and ask:

Q *Do all of your partner's notes make sense to you? If not, what can you ask your partner to help you understand?*

Q *If your partner is confused about something you wrote, how can you revise it to make what you mean clearer?*

Invite volunteers to share examples from their own writing as they answer these questions.

Reflect on Partner Work

Ask and briefly discuss:

Q *What did you do to work responsibly on your part of the work today? How did that help your pair work?*

Q *Did you and your partner disagree about anything today? If so, what did you do to reach agreement?*

Explain that partners will continue to work on their drafts next week.

Teacher Note

Save your grouped research notes and your model draft to use in Week 5.

Week 5 Overview

GENRE: EXPOSITORY NONFICTION

Writing Focus

- Students finish drafting their informational pieces.

- Students explore and integrate expository text features into their pieces.

- Students explore strong opening sentences.

- Students revise their writing with input from others.

- Students confer with one another and the teacher.

Social Focus

- Students make decisions and solve problems respectfully.

- Students act in fair and caring ways.

- Students help one another improve their writing.

- Students work in a responsible way.

- Students build on one another's thinking.

DO AHEAD

- Prior to Day 1, think about where you might add some text features (such as illustrations, captions, maps, headings, and boldfaced words connected to a glossary) to your model informational piece.

- Prior to Day 4, finish writing your model informational piece (from Week 4).

- Prior to Day 4, decide how you will combine pairs to form groups of four.

TEACHER AS WRITER

"To me, writing a book is a great voyage of discovery; what attracts me to a subject in part is what I don't know about it, what I can learn from it."
— David McCullough

Think about the subjects you are attracted to. What don't you know about those subjects? Write your reflections in your notebook.

Day 1

- *Life in the Rain Forests* from Week 1
- *Student Writing Handbook* pages 20–21
- Your draft informational piece from Week 4
- Loose, lined paper for writing drafts
- Chart paper and a marker
- A pad of small (1½" × 2") self-stick notes for each pair
- Unlined paper for text features

Drafting and Pair Conferring

In this lesson, the students:

- Explore and create expository text features
- Draft their informational piece
- Share the work fairly
- Reach agreement before making decisions
- Agree and disagree in a caring way
- Assess how a solution is working and modify it if necessary

GETTING READY TO WRITE

 Reread and Share Sentences

Gather the class with partners sitting together, facing you. Remind the students that last week they began drafting their nonfiction informational pieces. Review that the purpose of these pieces is to help their classmates become curious about their topics by writing about them in an interesting way.

Ask the students to quietly reread their own writing from last week and select one sentence that they feel might help others become curious about their topic. Tell them that you would like each student to read his sentence aloud. Ask the students to listen carefully to one another's sentences and to think about which ones make them curious.

Go around the room and have the students read their sentences aloud, without comment. When all have read, ask and briefly discuss:

Q *What sentences did you hear that make you curious?*

Explain that the students will continue to work on their drafts today, and encourage them to write in a way that helps others become as curious as they are about their topic.

 ## Explore Expository Text Features

Point out that nonfiction often includes various text features, such as maps and photographs, to provide additional information and to make the writing more interesting. Explain that the students will look closely at some of these features today and decide whether they want to include such features in their own informational pieces.

Show the cover of *Life in the Rain Forests*, and remind the students that they heard this book earlier in the unit. Ask them to open to *Student Writing Handbook* pages 20–21 as you show pages 6–7 of the book. Point out the expository text features on these pages (heading, map, boldfaced words, photographs, and captions). Ask the students to follow along as you read these pages aloud and to think about how these features help them understand the main text.

Read page 6 aloud, then point out that the shaded regions on the map show where rain forests are found today. Ask and briefly discuss:

Q *What information does the map provide that helps us understand the text?*

Q *What information does the heading provide that helps us understand the text?*

Write *map* and *heading* on a sheet of chart paper entitled "Text Features." Read page 7 aloud; then ask:

Q *What information do the photographs and captions provide that helps us understand the main text on page 6?*

Have a few volunteers share with the class; then add *photographs* and *captions* to the "Text Features" chart. Point out that the boldfaced words on page 6 (such as *environments*) are defined in the glossary on pages 30–31 of the book. Show the glossary and read a couple definitions aloud. Add *boldfaced words* and *glossary* to the chart.

Making Meaning® Teacher

The students have explored some of the text features in *Life in the Rain Forests* in *Making Meaning* Unit 2, Week 1. Take this opportunity to remind them of the features they listed on the "Text Features" chart from that week, looking at each feature again in the book. Then continue today's lesson at Step 3.

FACILITATION TIP

As you continue to focus on **pacing class discussions** this week, ask yourself:

- Do most students stay engaged for the duration of most discussions?

- What do the students look like when they are engaged? What do they look like when they become disengaged?

- What contributes to loss of focus on the part of the students?

- Are the students getting used to me not calling on every student with a hand up?

Continue to practice the techniques listed in the previous Facilitation Tip for speeding up or deepening a discussion.

Teacher Note ▶

You might say, "I might want to include a map of the Indian Ocean here to show which countries were hit by the great tsunami of 2004. I will write *map* on a self-stick note and place it here on my draft. I might also want to include an illustration that shows a wave next to a building to show my reader just how high a 50-foot wave is. I will write *illustration* on a self-stick note and mark this spot on my draft with it."

Teacher Note ▶

The students may write or draw their text features, copy them out of books, cut them out of magazines, or download them from the Internet.

3 ▶ Model Marking Your Draft for Text Features

Show and reread your draft informational piece. Think aloud about text features you might to include in your piece to give more information and help your readers understand the text. Point to each place in your draft where you might include a feature, and explain your thinking. Model writing the name of the text feature on a self-stick note and placing it where the feature will go.

4 ▶ Discuss Adding Text Features to Informational Pieces

Reread the items on the "Text Features" chart; then use "Think, Pair, Share" to have partners first think about and then discuss:

 Q *What text features might you want to include in your piece and why?* [pause] *Turn to your partner.*

After partners have talked, have a few pairs share their thinking with the class. Ask and briefly discuss:

Q *Where might you go for help in creating your text feature?*

Explain that today partners will decide what text features they want to include in their piece and begin creating them on separate sheets of paper. Point out that if they include photographs in their piece, they must include captions that tell about the photographs.

Explain that partners will decide where in their piece the text features will go and mark those places with self-stick notes. The note will remind them to leave space for that text feature when they copy their draft into its final version.

5 ▶ Discuss How Partners Will Work Together

Write the following tasks on the board and have partners work on them for 20–30 minutes.

- Decide what text features to include.

- Use self-stick notes to show where in their draft the text features will go.

- Continue drafting your informational piece.

- Begin creating text features for your piece.

Briefly discuss:

Q *Today you and your partner have many decisions to make. What have you learned about making decisions with a partner that will help you?*

Q *What are some ways to make a fair decision if you and your partner don't agree at first?*

Ask partners to spend a few minutes deciding what they want to accomplish today and how they will share the work fairly. Remind them that both partners need to be writing sections of their joint draft. When they are ready, have them return to their seats.

WRITING TIME

▶ **Draft Informational Pieces**

Have partners work on their informational pieces. As they work, circulate, observe, and offer assistance. When pairs seem to be working independently, confer with one pair at a time.

TEACHER CONFERENCE NOTE

As you did in Week 4, continue to confer with pairs about their informational piece. Ask partners to read their drafts aloud and to tell you their plan for their piece. Ask questions such as:

Q *What questions did you originally write that you will answer in your draft?*

Q *How did you categorize and order your notes? What made you decide to organize them that way?*

Q *What text features, if any, are you going to include? What information will you put in those features? Where will you put them?*

Q *How are you sharing the work fairly?*

Document your observations for each pair using the "Conference Notes" record sheet (BLM1).

Signal to let the students know when writing time is over.

7 ▶ Confer in Pairs and Reflect

As in Week 4, have partners read their writing from today to each other and check to make sure they each understand what the other has written. Give them time to clarify any confusion in their writing; then ask and briefly discuss:

Q *What text features have you and your partner decided to include? How did you decide?*

Q *What did you do to work responsibly on your part of the work today? How did that help your pair work?*

Q *Did you and your partner disagree about anything today? If so, what did you do to reach agreement?*

Explain that partners will continue to work on their pieces tomorrow.

Teacher Note

Save the "Text Features" chart to use on Day 2 and throughout the week.

Day 2

Drafting and Pair Conferring

Materials

- *Life in the Rain Forests*
- "Text Features" chart from Day 1
- Loose, lined paper for writing drafts
- Unlined paper for text features

In this lesson, the students:

- Explore and create expository text features
- Draft their informational piece
- Share the work fairly
- Reach agreement before making decisions

GETTING READY TO WRITE

▶ Briefly Review

Gather the class with partners sitting together, facing you. Review that they began thinking about text features to include in their informational pieces yesterday. Direct their attention to the "Text Features" chart and review the items on it. Ask and briefly discuss:

Q *Which text features are you and your partner planning to include in your piece? Tell us about them.*

Explain that the students will explore a few more text features and decide today if they want to include these features in their own pieces.

▶ Explore More Expository Text Features

Leaf through *Life in the Rain Forests* and draw the students' attention to the table of contents (page 3). Read it aloud and ask:

Q *Why might you want to include a table of contents?*

Add *table of contents* to the "Text Features" chart.

Follow this procedure to look at and discuss *diagrams with labels* (for example, page 4), *sidebars* (for example, "Did You Know?" on pages 4

Teacher Note ▶

If necessary, briefly explain how an index is organized and used.

and 18), and the *index* (page 32), each time adding the name of that feature to the chart.

3 ▶ **Discuss Adding Text Features to Informational Pieces**

Use "Think, Pair, Share" to have partners first think about and then discuss:

 Q *What other text features might you want to include in your piece and why?* [pause] *Turn to your partner.*

After partners have talked, have a few pairs share their thinking with the class. Explain that today partners will continue working on their drafts, including any text features they want to create. Remind them to use self-stick notes to show where a text feature will go when they write their final version.

4 ▶ **Discuss How Partners Will Work Together**

Write the following tasks on the board and have partners work on them for 20–30 minutes.

- Decide which additional text features you might want to include.

- Use self-stick notes to show where in your draft the text features will go.

- Continue drafting your informational piece.

- Continue creating text features for your piece.

Ask partners to spend a few minutes deciding what they will work on today and how they will share the work fairly. When they are ready, have them return to their seats and begin working.

WRITING TIME

5 ▶ **Draft Informational Pieces**

Have partners work on their informational pieces. As they work, circulate, observe, and offer assistance. When pairs seem to be working independently, confer with one pair at a time.

TEACHER CONFERENCE NOTE

Continue to confer with pairs about their informational piece. Ask partners to read their drafts aloud and to tell you their plan for their piece. Ask questions such as:

Q *What questions did you originally write that you will answer in your draft?*

Q *How did you categorize and order your notes? What made you decide to organize them that way?*

Q *What text features, if any, are you going to include? What information will you put in those features? Where will you put them?*

Q *How are you sharing the work fairly?*

Document your observations for each pair using the "Conference Notes" record sheet (BLM1).

Signal to let the students know when writing time is over.

SHARING AND REFLECTING

Confer in Pairs and Reflect

Have partners read their writing from today to each other and check to make sure they each understand what the other has written. Give them time to clarify any confusion in their writing; then ask and briefly discuss:

Q *What text features have you and your partner decided to include?*

Q *How are you sharing the work? Do you feel you are sharing it fairly? If not, what might you want to do differently tomorrow to share the work more fairly?*

Explain that partners will continue to work on their pieces tomorrow.

EXTENSION

Discuss Text Features in Other Nonfiction

Take time at the end of independent reading periods and other times during the day to discuss text features in the nonfiction students are reading. Have students share the title and author of the book they are reading and tell what the book is about. Discuss questions such as:

Q *What features (such as illustrations, captions, diagrams, graphs, tables of contents, and glossaries) of nonfiction do you see in your book?*

Q *How do those features give you more information or help you understand the text?*

Day 3

Analyzing and Revising Drafts

In this lesson, the students:

- Reread their writing critically
- Explore strong opening sentences
- Quick-write opening sentences that capture attention
- Get ideas by listening to others

GETTING READY TO WRITE

▶ Briefly Review

Have partners sit together at desks today. Review that they are working on drafts of their nonfiction informational pieces, which they will eventually publish for the class library. Yesterday they discussed text features they may want to include in their pieces.

Explain that in the next few days, you will help the students think about ways they can add to, revise, and improve their piece so it is as clear and interesting as possible for their readers.

Point out that in a nonfiction piece, as in all literature, a strong opening helps to get the reader's attention. Explain that the students will spend some time today looking at strong openings for nonfiction and will work on the opening sentences of their pieces.

▶ Discuss Strong Opening Sentences

Ask the students to open to *Student Writing Handbook* page 22, where the opening sentences from three books they heard earlier in the unit are reproduced. Ask them to follow along as you read the first passage aloud. Invite them to think about what the authors are doing in these openings to get readers interested in reading on.

Materials

- *Student Writing Handbook* page 22
- Your draft informational piece from Week 4
- Loose, lined paper for writing drafts
- Chart paper and a marker
- Unlined paper for text features

Read the first passage aloud twice:

> "A raging wildfire is a frightening thing. Living trees burn as fast as cardboard boxes in a bonfire. Flames race through treetops, sometimes faster than a person can run, burning at temperatures hot enough to melt steel." (from *Wildfires*)

Ask:

Q *What do you think the author is doing in these opening sentences to get us interested in reading this book? Turn to your partner.*

Signal for attention and have a few volunteers share their thinking with the class.

> **Students might say:**
>
> "I think the words 'faster than a person can run' makes us imagine what it might be like to be caught in a wildfire."
>
> "Maybe the author wants us to feel a little scared."

Repeat this procedure with the next two passages:

> "The earth beneath our feet usually feels solid and firm. Yet a million times each year—an average of once every thirty seconds—somewhere around the world the ground shakes and sways." (from *Earthquake*)

> "Imagine a forest unchanged for 60 million years, where giant trees reach up to the sky, their leafy branches blocking out light to the forest floor below." (from *Life in the Rain Forests*)

Point out that all three authors introduce their topic using opening sentences that are descriptive and that help the reader imagine something interesting about their topic.

 3 Model Writing a Strong Opening

Direct the students' attention to your model informational piece from Week 4. Reread the piece aloud; then ask:

Q *Do you think my current opening is successful at getting the reader's attention? Why or why not?*

Q *What other opening sentences could I write to introduce my topic and capture my reader's attention?*

Use the students' suggestions to write several possible opening sentences for your piece on a sheet of chart paper. You might try writing some sentences that are similar to the ones the students explored in Step 2 (for example, *Imagine an ocean wave taller than your school. It sweeps in and washes everything away—people, buildings, pets, trees, and cars. This has really happened. These waves are called tsunamis*).

▶ Quick-Write: Possible Opening Sentences

Ask partners to reread the sections they have written so far. After a moment, use "Think, Pair, Share" to have partners first think about, and then discuss:

Q *What opening sentences might you write to introduce your topic and capture your reader's attention?* [pause] *Turn to your partner.*

After partners have had a chance to talk, signal for their attention. Have them open to the next blank page in their notebooks and do a 5-minute quick-write together in which they will write at least three different ways they could begin their piece.

After 5 minutes, signal for attention and have a few volunteers share a possible opening sentence with the class.

Explain that partners may use one of the opening sentences they just wrote to begin their piece, or they may write another one. Encourage them to keep working until they agree on an opening that they believe will capture their reader's attention.

▶ Discuss How Partners Will Work Together

Write the following tasks on the board and have partners work on them for 20–30 minutes.

- Add a strong opening to your piece.

- Draft your informational piece, including any text features.

- Share the work fairly.

Ask partners to spend a few minutes deciding what they will work on today, and how they will share the work fairly. When they are ready, have them begin working.

WRITING TIME

6 ▶ Draft Informational Pieces

Have partners work together on their informational pieces. As they work, circulate, observe, and offer assistance. When pairs seem to be working independently, confer with one pair at a time.

TEACHER CONFERENCE NOTE

Continue to confer with pairs about their informational piece. Ask partners to read their drafts aloud and to tell you their plan for their piece. Ask questions such as:

Q *What questions did you originally write that you will answer in your draft?*

Q *How did you categorize and order your notes? What made you decide to organize them that way?*

Q *What text features, if any, are you going to include? What information will you put in those features? Where will you put them?*

Q *How are you sharing the work fairly?*

Q *Do you think your opening will capture the reader's attention? Why or why not? How might you revise it to be more [scary/interesting/exciting]?*

Document your observations for each pair using the "Conference Notes" record sheet (BLM1).

Signal to let the students know when writing time is over.

SHARING AND REFLECTING

▶ Share Opening Sentences and Reflect

Explain that each pair will read its opening sentence aloud to the class. Give pairs a moment to decide which partner will read their opening sentence aloud. Go around the room and have each pair read its opening sentence, without comment.

When all pairs have shared their sentence, ask and briefly discuss:

Q *What opening sentences did you hear that captured your attention?*

Q *What ideas did you get about your own opening sentences from hearing other people's sentences?*

Explain that pairs will get feedback about their informational pieces from another pair tomorrow.

Day 4

Materials

- Completed draft of your informational piece
- Chart paper and a marker
- *Assessment Resource Book*

Group Conferring

In this lesson, the students:

- Ask for and receive feedback about their writing
- Give feedback in a helpful way
- Ask one another questions about their writing
- Discuss and solve problems that arise in their work together
- Include one another and contribute to group work

GETTING READY TO WRITE

1 ▶ Prepare for Group Conferences

Explain that today each pair will meet with another pair to confer about their informational pieces (see "Do Ahead" on page 437). They will share their drafts and get feedback from the other pair about anything confusing or unclear; then they will make any necessary revisions until they are convinced that their pieces make sense and are complete.

Remind the students that in the writing community the goal of giving feedback is to help each person create the best possible piece of writing. In pairs and as a class, discuss:

 Q *What have you learned about giving feedback respectfully? Turn to your partner.*

Q *What problems can arise when giving feedback? How will you avoid those problems today?*

Prepare to Give Feedback: Does It All Make Sense?

Explain that, as the students listen to one another's writing, you would like them to ask themselves the three questions that follow. Write the questions on a sheet of chart paper as you say them aloud:

- Does this writing make sense? Can I track what the author is saying?
- Is there anywhere I am confused? Where?
- What have I heard in this piece that makes me curious?

Help the students practice giving feedback about these three questions by showing your model informational piece and reading it aloud, along with any revisions. Use "Think, Pair, Share" to have partners consider and discuss the three questions about your draft. Then have several volunteers give you feedback about your draft using the three questions.

Encourage the students to listen carefully to their group members and to be ready to report the feedback they heard to the class.

Confer in Groups

Have pairs move into the groups you have assigned. Give them ample time to confer.

CLASS ASSESSMENT NOTE

Circulate among conferring groups and observe the conferences. Ask yourself:

- Are groups staying on task, reading and discussing their writing?

continues

> CLASS ASSESSMENT NOTE *continued*
>
> • Are group members asking each other questions about their drafts?
>
> • Are they giving each other feedback in a helpful and respectful way?
>
> Make note of any problems you notice groups having to bring up during the reflection discussion.
>
> Record your observations in the *Assessment Resource Book*.

When most groups have had time to discuss their drafts, call for the class's attention.

4 ▸ Reflect on Feedback Received

Ask and briefly discuss as a class:

Q *What did the members of your group do to be respectful during your conference?*

Remind the students that when authors receive feedback they may or may not agree with all of the feedback. Authors decide which feedback they will use. Use "Think, Pair, Share" to have partners first think about and then discuss:

 Q *What feedback did you hear today that you might use when you rewrite your draft?* [pause] *Turn to your partner.*

 Q *What feedback do you want to think more about before deciding whether to use it or not?* [pause] *Turn to your partner.*

5 ▸ Discuss How Partners Will Work Together

Explain that today partners will work together to make any agreed-upon revisions and reread their drafts to make sure it is as clear, interesting, and complete as it can be.

Ask partners to spend a few minutes deciding what they will work on today and how they will share the work. When they are ready, have them return to their seats and begin working.

WRITING TIME

▶ **Finish Drafts**

Have pairs work on finishing their drafts. As they work, circulate, observe, and offer assistance. When pairs seem to be working independently, confer with pairs.

TEACHER CONFERENCE NOTE

Continue to confer with pairs about their informational piece. Ask partners to read their drafts aloud and to tell you their plan for their piece. Ask questions such as:

Q *What questions did you originally write that you will answer in your draft?*

Q *How did you categorize and order your notes? What made you decide to organize them that way?*

Q *What text features, if any, are you going to include? What information will you put in those features? Where will you put them?*

Q *How are you sharing the work fairly?*

Q *Do you think your opening will capture the reader's attention? Why or why not? How might you revise it to be more [scary/interesting/exciting]?*

Document your observations for each pair using the "Conference Notes" record sheet (BLM1).

Signal to let the students know when writing time is over.

7 ▶ **Briefly Reflect on Writing**

Help the students reflect on their work today by briefly discussing:

Q *What feedback did you incorporate into your draft today? Tell us about it.*

Explain that pairs will publish their final version next week.

EXTENSION

Teach Cooperative Structures for Group Work

Look for opportunities throughout the school day for students to work in groups of four (or three or five, if necessary). Two cooperative structures you can teach them to use in group work are "Heads Together" and "Group Brainstorming." These are described in the front matter in volume 1 on page xiv. Group work can be more challenging for students than pair work. Take time to discuss problems, as well as how group members are including one another and contributing responsibly to the work.

Teacher Note ▶

If many pairs still need time to finish writing their drafts, give them an opportunity to do this before moving on to Week 6.

Week 6 Overview

GENRE: EXPOSITORY NONFICTION

Writing Focus

- Students write the final version of their informational piece.

- Students explore transition words to connect ideas.

- Students proofread for spelling and punctuation errors.

- Students present their informational piece to the class from the Author's Chair.

- Students confer with one another and the teacher.

Social Focus

- Students make decisions and solve problems respectfully.

- Students act in fair and caring ways.

- Students express interest in and appreciation for one another's writing.

- Students give their full attention to the person who is speaking.

DO AHEAD

- Prior to Day 1, decide how pairs will publish their final version for the class library. For example, each pair might make a book (see the note on page 136 in volume 1 for bookmaking resources) or make a poster with the final version attached to it. Gather any necessary materials.

- Prior to Day 1, decide whether you will have the students handwrite or use a computer to generate their final versions. You may want to recruit parents or older students to help with word processing on and printing from computers.

TEACHER AS WRITER

"I get pieces, flashes of an idea, an image, and I won't know what it means, but I'll be fascinated by it. It's all there in that first instant—it's complete—but all I know is the wonder and the curiosity."
— *Mekeel McBride*

Think about the informational piece you have written as a model for the students over the past few weeks. What have you learned about the topic as you researched and wrote about it? What surprised you? What are you curious about now? Jot your reflections in your notebook, and consider writing more about this topic at a later time.

Day 1

Materials

- Transparencies of "Passages About Sharks" (BLM19–BLM20)
- *Student Writing Handbooks* pages 23–25
- Loose, lined paper for final versions
- Other materials for publishing informational pieces (see "Do Ahead" on page 457)
- *Assessment Resource Book*

Writing Final Versions

In this lesson, the students:

- Reread their writing critically
- Explore transition words to connect ideas
- Analyze their draft for transitions
- Begin writing their final version

GETTING READY TO WRITE

 Briefly Review

Have partners sit together at desks today. Explain that this week they will work on the final version of their informational piece. They will publish it by sharing it with the class from the Author's Chair and placing it in the class library.

Remind the students that last week they thought about how to capture the reader's attention with a strong opening. Explain that, after getting their reader's attention, it is equally important to keep this attention by making sure their ideas are connected and make sense together. Explain that authors use *transition words* (sometimes called *conjunctions*) to help readers connect one idea to another in a piece of writing.

 Discuss Transition Words

Show the transparencies of "Passages About Sharks" (1 and 2) as you ask the students to turn to *Student Writing Handbook* pages 23–24, where the passages are reproduced. Have them follow along as you read the first passage aloud. (If necessary, read it twice.) Point out the transition words in boldface and explain that *while*, *perhaps to*, *usually*, and *other times* are all words that connect ideas in the passage.

In grade 5, the students begin exploring conjunctions and transitions in an informal way—as words that connect ideas. This lays the foundation for more formal experience with this grammar in later grades. In this lesson, they are simply introduced to some examples of words that connect ideas and are invited to try incorporating some of them into their own writing.

Reread the first sentence aloud and point out that the word *while* connects the idea that great whites do strange things and the idea that they are hunting. Reread the second sentence aloud; then ask:

Q *What two ideas are connected by the words* perhaps to *in this sentence? Turn to your partner.*

If necessary, point out that *perhaps to* connects the idea that sharks have been seen poking their heads out of the water with the idea that they are looking for seals sunning themselves.

Repeat this question for the words *usually* and *other times*. Point out that transition words can appear at the beginning or middle of a sentence.

Repeat this procedure with the second passage, discussing the words *when*, *but*, and *although*. Have the students turn to handbook page 25 and explain that this is a list of some common transition words used in the English language. Read them aloud together.

▶ Review Drafts

Ask the students to reread their drafts and think quietly to themselves about the following questions:

Q *What transition words, if any, have you used to connect ideas in your piece?*

Q *Where else might you be able to use a transition word to connect ideas in your piece?*

Have partners talk about their thinking for a few minutes; then have a few volunteers share with the class.

Explain that partners will review their draft to see if they can add any transition words; then they will begin working on their final versions by copying their drafts on loose, lined paper. Remind the students to write in their best handwriting and to leave space for their text features. Encourage them to keep their handbooks open to page 25 today and try to include some of the transition words in their writing if they can.

Teacher Note

If necessary, point out that *usually* connects the idea that researchers have photographed great whites jumping out of the water with the idea that sharks were attacking their natural prey. *Other times* connects the idea that sharks usually jumped when they were attacking their natural prey and the idea that they were chasing plastic decoys towed behind boats.

Teacher Note

If necessary, point out that *when* connects the idea that great whites visit the three coasts with the idea that seals, sea lions, and elephant seals come onto land to give birth. *But* connects the idea that the sharks roam all the world's oceans with the idea that they aren't common anywhere. *Although* connects the idea that great whites will come together to feed on the same prey with the idea that they don't usually travel together.

4▶ Discuss How Partners Will Work Together

Write the following tasks on the board and have partners work on them for 20–30 minutes.

- Review your draft and add transition words if you can.

- Begin copying your draft into its final version, leaving space for text features.

- Share the work fairly.

Ask partners to spend a few minutes deciding how they will share the work fairly. Remind them that both partners are responsible for writing sections of their final piece. When they are ready, have them begin working.

WRITING TIME

5▶ Write Final Versions of Informational Pieces

Have partners work on the final versions of their informational pieces. As they work, circulate and observe.

> ### CLASS ASSESSMENT NOTE
>
> Observe pairs working and ask yourself:
>
> - Are partners working together to write a final version of their informational piece?
>
> - Are they sharing the work fairly?
>
> Support struggling pairs by asking them questions such as:
>
> **Q** *What are each of you responsible for accomplishing during this writing time?*
>
> **Q** *Is the way you are sharing the work fair? Why or why not? [What can you do to make it so you are sharing the work fairly?]*
>
> *continues*

CLASS ASSESSMENT NOTE *continued*

Q *Why is it important that both of you do your part of the work on this project?*

Record your observations in the *Assessment Resource Book*.

Signal to let the students know when writing time is over.

SHARING AND REFLECTING

▶ Reflect and "Preview" Pieces as a Class

Explain that each pair will give the class a "preview" of their informational piece by reading any two sentences aloud from it. Ask partners to quietly reread their piece and select two interesting sentences (one for each partner) to read aloud. Give them a few moments to select their sentences and then ask the class to listen carefully to one another's sentences and to think about which ones make them curious.

Go around the room and have the students read their sentences aloud, without comment. When all have read, ask and briefly discuss:

Q *What sentences did you hear that made you curious?*

Remind the students that they will hear one another's completed pieces from the Author's Chair later this week. Explain that pairs will continue to work on their final versions tomorrow.

Day 2

Materials

- Transparency of "Unpunctuated Nonfiction Paragraph" (BLM21)
- Overhead pen
- *Student Writing Handbook* page 26, word bank, and proofreading notes sections
- Loose, lined paper for final versions
- Other materials for publishing informational pieces
- *Assessment Resource Book*

Writing Final Versions and Proofreading

In this lesson, the students:

- Practice punctuating text
- Proofread for spelling, grammar, and punctuation
- Listen for periods as they read their drafts aloud
- Work on their final version for publication

GETTING READY TO WRITE

 Briefly Review

Gather the class with partners sitting together, facing you. Explain that today partners will work on finishing the final version of their informational piece. Remind the students that the purpose of these informational pieces is to help their classmates become interested in, and curious about, the topics they selected to research. Explain that their pieces need to be as correct as possible so their classmates can read and understand them easily. Today they will proofread their pieces to make sure they have corrected all errors.

 Proofreading: Listening for Periods

As a class, practice listening for and punctuating the ends of sentences by showing the transparency of the "Unpunctuated Nonfiction Paragraph" and asking the students to follow along on *Student Writing Handbook* page 26 as you read it aloud. Read the passage without pauses. Ask:

Q *What's strange about the way I read this passage?*

Point out that right now the passage is one long sentence—which doesn't sound right when read aloud. Ask the students to slowly reread the passage with you and to stop when it feels natural to do so. At each stop (and as appropriate), model writing a comma or a period and capitalizing, where appropriate, to begin a new sentence. Ask the students to do the same in their handbooks.

Explain that you would like the students to read their own drafts aloud today to make sure they have used periods, commas, and other punctuation marks as appropriate.

Review Using the Word Bank and Proofreading Notes

Remind the students that they should use their word bank and proofreading notes to help them proofread their drafts for spelling and correctness. Briefly review these procedures by reminding the students to:

- Circle words in their drafts that they are unsure how to spell, and look them up in their word bank. Add any words that are not already in their word bank after looking them up in a dictionary or other source.

- Use their proofreading notes as a list of things to check in their drafts before publishing. Correct any errors by crossing out the error in the draft and writing the correction next to it.

Remind the students to correct any misspellings or errors they may have copied into their final versions yesterday.

Discuss How Partners Will Work Together

Explain the following tasks as you write them on the board:

- Reread your draft aloud and check for correct sentence punctuation.

- Proofread for spelling, using the word bank.

- Proofread correctness, using the proofreading notes.

- Finish writing your final version, including text features.

Ask partners to spend a few minutes deciding what they will work on today and how they will share the work fairly. When they are ready, have them return to their seats and begin working.

Teacher Note

To provide your students with more practice with listening for periods and punctuating text, do the related activities in the *Skill Practice Teaching Guide* with them.

WRITING TIME

5 ▶ **Proofread and Write Final Versions**

Have pairs work on proofreading and writing their final versions. Circulate, observe, and offer assistance as they work.

CLASS ASSESSMENT NOTE

Observe pairs working and ask yourself:

- Are partners working together fairly to write a final version of their informational piece?

- Are they catching and correcting spelling, grammar, and punctuation errors?

Support struggling pairs by asking them questions such as:

Q *What are each of you responsible for accomplishing during this writing time?*

Q *Is the way you are sharing the work fair? Why or why not? [What can you do to make it so you are sharing the work fairly?]*

Q *Why is it important that both of you do your part of the work on this project?*

Record your observations in the *Assessment Resource Book*.

Signal to let the students know when writing time is over.

SHARING AND REFLECTING

6 ▶ **Reflect on Proofreading**

Ask and briefly discuss:

Q *What words did you find in your word bank today? How did you check on words that were not in the word bank?*

Q *What corrections did you make in your draft after reviewing your proofreading notes?*

Explain that the students will finish their pieces tomorrow and begin sharing them from the Author's Chair.

EXTENSION

Learn How to Cite Resources in a Bibliography

Explain that nonfiction texts commonly include a bibliography—a list of books and other resources for readers to explore if they'd like to read more about the topic. Find some examples of bibliographies in your collected nonfiction resources to show and discuss with the students. Read a few of the book citations aloud and point out that each book is identified by title, author's name, where it was published, the name of the publishing company, and the year it was published (copyright date).

Explain that the students may want to include a bibliography in their informational piece. If so, they will need to know how to correctly cite the resources in alphabetical order. Model writing a book citation for one of the read-aloud books from this unit. Show the students where to find the publisher and place of publication (on the title page) and the copyright date (usually the copyright page). Call their attention to how you are punctuating the citation. For example:

Simon, Seymour. *Earthquakes*. New York, NY: HarperCollins, 1991.

Repeat this procedure to model writing citations for magazines and websites. Examples include:

Margolis, Marc. "Reefs." *Newsweek* Oct. 2006; pp. 32–34.

"Tsunami" from Wikipedia, www.wikipedia.com

Day 3

Materials

- Materials for publishing informational pieces
- Two chairs to use for Author's Chair sharing

Writing Final Versions and Publishing

In this lesson, the students:

- Finish writing their final version, including any text features
- Handle materials responsibly and share them fairly
- Make decisions about how they will present their pieces from the Author's Chair
- Express interest in and appreciation for one another's writing
- Ask one another questions about their writing

GETTING READY TO WRITE

 1 ▶ Discuss Handling and Sharing Materials

Have partners sit together at desks today. Explain that partners will finish working on the final version of their informational piece, including any text features. Pairs who finish will begin sharing their pieces from the Authors' Chairs today.

Briefly discuss how the students are doing with sharing materials and equipment fairly, handling them responsibly, and helping one another as they finish their final pieces. Ask and briefly discuss:

Q *What will you do to take care of our [bookmaking] materials? Why is that important?*

Q *What have you been doing to share equipment like the computers or the hole-punch? Has that been fair? If not, what can we do today to share those things more fairly?*

Encourage the students to think about how they are sharing the materials fairly as they work today.

WRITING TIME

▶ Finish Final Versions of Informational Pieces

Have pairs work on finishing their informational pieces. If partners finish, have them talk about and decide how they will present their informational piece to the class (for example, who will read what sections aloud).

As pairs work, circulate, observe, and offer assistance.

Signal to let the students know when writing time is over.

SHARING AND REFLECTING

▶ Review Sharing Writing from the Author's Chair

Gather the class with partners sitting together, facing the Authors' Chairs. If necessary, remind them of the procedure you established for presenting books from the Authors' Chairs (see Unit 2, Week 3, Day 4, pages 142–143).

Before asking a pair to share from the Authors' Chairs today, discuss how the students will act, both as presenting authors and as members of the audience. Ask and discuss:

Q *Why is it important to speak in a loud, clear voice when you're reading your piece to the class?*

Q *If you're in the audience and you can't hear the author, how can you politely let him or her know?*

Q *How will you let the authors know that you're interested in their piece? Why is it important to express interest in one another's writing?*

Encourage the students to be attentive and considerate audience members, and tell them that you will check in with them afterward to see how they did.

ELL Note

Support trios as necessary to make sure that all three students in each trio have a role in presenting their piece to the class.

Conduct Author's Chair Sharing

Ask a pair who has finished publishing its informational piece to read the piece aloud from the Authors' Chairs. At the end of the sharing, facilitate a discussion using questions like those that follow, and give the authors an opportunity to respond to the class's comments and questions:

Q *What did you learn about [condors] from hearing [Dante and Thuy's] piece?*

Q *What are you curious about after hearing their piece?*

Q *What questions can we ask [Dante and Thuy] about their piece?*

Follow this procedure and have other pairs share from Authors' Chairs as time permits.

 Reflect on Audience Behavior During Author's Chair Sharing

Ask and briefly discuss:

Q *What did we do well as an audience today? What might we want to work on the next time authors share their work?*

Q *If you shared a piece today, how did the audience make you feel? What did they do that made you feel [relaxed/nervous/proud]?*

Place the informational pieces in the class library after they are read aloud so students can read them on their own during independent reading time. Explain that tomorrow pairs who have not finished publishing will have time to do so and that more pairs will share their piece from the Authors' Chairs.

EXTENSION

Technology Tip: Publishing Student Writing Online

This week the students are publishing their nonfiction for the class library. Some students might also be interested in publishing their writing online. There are a number of websites where students can publish their writing online; search for them using the keywords "publishing children's writing." Publishing online allows family members and friends to easily access and enjoy students' writing.

Day 4

Materials

- Materials for publishing informational pieces
- Two chairs to use for Author's Chair sharing

Writing Final Versions and Publishing

In this lesson, the students:

- Review and reflect on writing nonfiction
- Finish publishing their pieces
- Present their pieces from the Authors' Chairs
- Express interest in and appreciation for one another's writing
- Ask one another questions about their writing
- Give their full attention to the person who is speaking

GETTING READY TO WRITE

 1 Review and Reflect on Writing Nonfiction

Have partners sit together at desks today. Remind the students that over the past six weeks they have learned about writing nonfiction and have researched and written a nonfiction piece about a topic they were curious about. Ask:

Q *What have you learned about writing nonfiction over the past weeks*

> **Students might say:**
>
> "I learned that you can write about things you are curious about."
>
> "I agree with [Brad]. I learned that you can find out about things by researching them."
>
> "In addition to what [Jackie] said, I learned that you can take notes and use them in your nonfiction writing."
>
> "I learned ways to capture the reader's attention and make the reader curious about my topic."

Have partners use "Think, Pair, Share" to first think about and then discuss each of the following questions:

Q *What was your favorite part of working on your informational piece?* [pause] *Turn to your partner.*

Q *What is one thing you are glad you learned about writing nonfiction?* [pause] *Turn to your partner.*

Q *What did you find challenging about writing nonfiction?* [pause] *Turn to your partner.*

Remind the students that writers become better over time as they practice writing again and again. Encourage students who feel drawn to nonfiction to continue to research and write about nonfiction topics they are interested in during their free time and during the open weeks of this program.

Explain that today partners will finish publishing their piece and then decide and practice how they will present it to the class. Those who finish may write anything they choose during writing time.

Explain that after writing time, more pairs will share their pieces with the class from the Authors' Chairs. Ask partners to spend a few minutes deciding what they will accomplish and how they will share their work today.

WRITING TIME

▶ Finish Publishing Pieces and Prepare to Share

Have pairs work on publishing and preparing to share for 10–15 minutes. Circulate, observe, and offer assistance.

Signal to let the students know when writing time is over.

SHARING AND REFLECTING

 Conduct Author's Chair Sharing

Gather the class with partners sitting together, facing the Authors' Chairs. Remind them to speak in a loud, clear voice and to show interest in and appreciation for their classmates' writing.

Have a pair read its piece aloud from the Authors' Chairs. At the end of the sharing, facilitate a discussion using questions like those that follow, and give the authors an opportunity to respond to the class comments and questions:

Q   *What did you learn about [global warming] from hearing [Cara and Tomas's] piece?*

Q   *What are you curious about after hearing their piece?*

Q   *What questions can we ask [Cara and Tomas] about their piece?*

Repeat this procedure to have other pairs share from the Authors' Chairs, as time permits.

Assure the students that pairs who haven't yet shared will get to share their published informational piece from the Authors' Chairs in the coming days.

After the informational pieces are read aloud, place them in the class library so students can read them during independent reading time.

 Reflect on Interactions and Thank One Another

Ask and briefly discuss:

Q   *What did we do well as an audience today? What do we still want to work on the next time authors share their work?*

Q   *If you shared a piece today, how did the audience make you feel? What did they do that made you feel [relaxed/nervous/proud]?*

Teacher Note

If necessary, repeat today's lesson for a few more days, or even another week, to give all the pairs time to finish publishing their pieces (see Open Weeks in the front matter on volume 1, page xvi). Students who finish may begin a new piece of writing (nonfiction or otherwise) or continue working on a piece of writing they started earlier.

Even if you decide to begin another genre unit immediately, continue to have pairs share their nonfiction informational pieces from the Authors' Chairs until everyone has had a chance to do so.

Point out that partners have worked closely together for several weeks to research and write about the topic they chose. Ask and briefly discuss:

Q   *In what ways did you and your partner help each other on this project?*

Q   *What do you appreciate about how your partner worked with you? Turn and tell your partner.*

Ask partners to take a moment to thank each other for their help and collaboration.

Teacher Note

This is the last week of the expository nonfiction unit. You will need to reassign partners before beginning the next unit.

EXTENSION

Write Letters Home About Nonfiction

Provide letter-writing practice for the students by having them write a letter home about what they learned about nonfiction from working on their informational pieces. Discuss questions such as:

Q   *What's special about nonfiction writing?*

Q   *What steps did you and your partner go through to research and write about your topic?*

Q   *What is one thing you're proud of about your published informational piece?*

If necessary, review the elements of a letter (date, salutation, body, closing, and signature) by modeling or writing a shared sample letter with the class. Have the students write and proofread their letters; then attach each student's letter to a copy of the published informational piece he helped to write and send it home.

Persuasive Nonfiction

Persuasive Nonfiction

Genre

Persuasive Nonfiction

During this three-week unit, the students read and write essays defending particular opinions as they explore the elements of persuasive essays. They brainstorm topics they have strong opinions about and select one of those topics to write a persuasive essay about. They learn to identify an audience for their essay and they state and support their opinions with reasons. They confer in pairs and revise their essays based on partner feedback. Socially, they express their own opinions as they learn to respect and consider the opinions of others. They also express interest in and appreciation for one another's writing.

Development Across the Grades

Grade	Elements of Persuasive Nonfiction	Language and Craft	Skills and Conventions
5	• Generating opinions and choosing topics • Identifying the purpose and audience of persuasive nonfiction • Using reasons to support opinions	• Writing clear statements of opinion • Exploring strong openings and conclusions	• Exploring the use of commas in direct quotations • Listening for periods • Proofreading drafts for spelling, punctuation, and grammar
6	• Generating opinions and choosing topics • Identifying the purpose and audience of persuasive nonfiction • Using reasons to support opinions	• Writing clear statements of opinion • Exploring strong openings and conclusions	• Exploring the use of commas in direct quotations • Listening for periods • Proofreading drafts for spelling, punctuation, and grammar

UNIT OVERVIEW

WEEK	DAY 1	DAY 2	DAY 3	DAY 4
	Immersion and Drafting			
1	**Exploring Persuasive Writing:** "WARNING: Too Much TV Is Hazardous to Your Health" **Focus:** What is the author trying to do?	**Exploring Persuasive Writing:** "Television: The Most Disparaged Resource of the Information Age" **Focus:** Purpose and audience	**Exploring Persuasive Writing:** "Animal Experimentation Saves Lives" **Quick-Write:** Opinions	**Exploring Persuasive Writing:** "Animal Testing: Here Is the Truth" **Focus:** Brainstorm topics for persuasive essays
2	**Exploring Persuasive Writing:** "School Uniforms" **Focus:** Choosing an opinion and audience for a persuasive essay	**Drafting Persuasive Essays** **Focus:** Strong opening and clear statement of opinion	**Drafting Persuasive Essays** **Focus:** Giving reasons to support opinions	**Drafting Persuasive Essays** **Focus:** Concluding persuasive essays
	Revision, Proofreading, and Publication			
3	**Pair Conferring and Revising** **Focus:** Does it make sense?	**Proofreading** **Focus:** Commas in direct quotations	**Publishing** **Focus:** Author's Chair sharing	**Publishing** **Focus:** Publishing for class and a wider audience

GENRE: PERSUASIVE NONFICTION

"WARNING: Too Much TV Is Hazardous to Your Health"
adapted from www.tvturnoff.org
(see page 499)

Television contributes to decreases in family time and academic performance while contributing to increases in violence and obesity.

"Television: The Most Disparaged Resource of the Information Age"
adapted from essay by Salmaan S. on www.teenink.com
(see page 501)

Television is a valuable source of information that unites humankind.

"Animal Experimentation Saves Lives"
adapted from essay by Giovanny P. on www.teenink.com
(see page 502)

Advances in health and medicine justify sacrificing animals in the lab.

"Animal Testing: Here Is the Truth"
adapted from essay by Emma H. on www.teenink.com
(see page 503)

Animal experimentation is cruel and inhuman; alternatives are available.

Writing Focus

- Students hear and discuss persuasive essays.

- Students identify the purpose and audience for persuasive essays.

- Students think about what information is communicated in persuasive essays.

- Students generate opinions they feel strongly about for persuasive essays.

Social Focus

- Students listen respectfully to the thinking of others and share their own.

- Students work in a responsible way.

DO AHEAD

- Prior to Day 1, decide how you will randomly assign partners to work together during the unit. See the front matter in volume 1 for suggestions about assigning partners randomly (see page xiii) and for considerations for pairing English Language Learners (see page xxviii).

- Consider prereading and discussing this week's read-aloud selections with your English Language Learners. Stop during the reading to discuss vocabulary and check for understanding. (See ELL vocabulary listed in the lessons.)

TEACHER AS WRITER

"Write about what bugs you."
— *Tennessee Williams*

In this unit the students explore the genre of persuasive essay—essays intended to persuade the reader of the author's opinion through well-thought-out argument and evidence. Many persuasive essays arise from an author's sense that something is amiss and needs to be addressed or corrected.

Make a list of topics that "bug" you about your own life, community, country, or world. What bugs you about these things? Are they unfair? Inconvenient? Wrong in other ways? Jot some notes about your thoughts in your notebook.

Day 1

Materials

- "WARNING: Too Much TV Is Hazardous to Your Health" (see pages 499–500)
- *Student Writing Handbook* pages 27–28

Exploring Persuasive Writing

In this lesson, the students:

- Work with a new partner
- Share what they learn about their partner
- Hear and discuss a persuasive essay
- Think about the author's purpose
- Write about things that interest them

About Persuasive Writing

In this unit, the students learn that the purpose of a persuasive essay is to persuade the reader of the author's opinion. They identify topics they have strong opinions about and think about who the intended audience of a persuasive essay might be. They explore how essays can be structured as they learn to state an opinion in the opening paragraph, support their opinion in subsequent paragraphs, and reaffirm their opinion in closing. The students learn that many published persuasive essays contain researched facts and data to support a given position, although they are not expected to extensively research their topic in grade 5. However, you might wish to incorporate a stronger research focus into this unit by having the students find data and other information about their topics to support their positions. If so, be ready to help them find resources about their topics at the library or on the Internet.

In this unit, the students publish one persuasive essay for a class collection, and they consider ways to publish their essays for a wider audience beyond the classroom.

Teacher Note

The partners you assign today will stay together for the unit.

Making Meaning® Teacher

You can either have the students work with their current *Making Meaning* partner or assign them a new partner for this unit.

GETTING READY TO WRITE

 Pair Students and Discuss Working Together

Randomly assign partners (see "Do Ahead" on page 479) and let them know that they will work together on their writing for the coming three weeks. Gather them with partners sitting together, facing you. Ask them to bring their *Student Writing Handbooks* with them.

Have partners take a couple of minutes to get to know each other by talking about some of the things they have written so far this year; then signal for their attention. Ask and briefly discuss:

Q *What did you learn about the writing your partner has done this year?*

Q *What have you learned about working with someone else that will help you in working with your new partner?*

Read "WARNING: Too Much TV Is Hazardous to Your Health" Aloud

Explain that in this unit the students will focus on writing a special kind of nonfiction. Tell them that you will read a short essay (or piece of nonfiction writing) aloud. Invite them to think about what the author might be trying to do in this essay.

Without identifying it as a persuasive essay, read "WARNING: Too Much TV Is Hazardous to Your Health" aloud slowly and clearly, clarifying vocabulary as you read.

◀ **Teacher Note**

To review the procedure for defining vocabulary during the read-aloud, see volume 1, page 8.

Suggested Vocabulary

negative consequences: bad things that happen as a result of something

excessive: too much

sedentary lifestyles: a way of living without enough exercise

obesity: state of being very overweight

decade: ten years

diminished: went down

promotes: encourages

positive correlation: relationship

ELL Vocabulary

English Language Learners may benefit from discussing additional vocabulary, including:

an abundance of evidence: lots of reasons

harms: hurts

reduce inactivity: get more active

Ask and briefly discuss:

Q *What is the author trying to do in this essay?*

▶3 Reread the Essay and Discuss the Author's Purpose

Have the students open to *Student Writing Handbook* page 27–28, where the essay is reproduced. Point out that this essay is adapted from a website called www.tvturnoff.org. Ask the students to reread the essay with their partner and to think about what the author is trying to convince them about.

After partners have had a chance to read the essay, signal for their attention. Ask and briefly discuss:

Q *What is the author trying to convince us about? How do you know?*

Q *Why does it make sense that this essay would appear on a website called "www.tvturnoff.org"?*

Q *Does this essay convince you? Why or why not?*

> **Students might say:**
>
> "I think the author is trying to convince us not to watch too much TV."
>
> "I agree with [Paula]. The author gives lots and lots of reasons why it's not good for people, especially kids."
>
> "I am convinced because the author put in quotes by scientists."
>
> "I disagree with [Trent]. I'm not convinced that I watch too much TV."

If necessary, point out that the author is trying to persuade, or convince, the reader that watching too much TV is harmful, especially for children. The author states a clear opinion in the first paragraph ("our television habit has serious negative consequences") and gives several reasons that support that opinion in the paragraphs that follow. Explain that this kind of nonfiction writing is called *persuasive essay* and that the students will spend the next few weeks exploring and learning to write persuasive essays. Ask:

Q *Why might it be good to know how to write a persuasive essay?*

Teacher Note

Regularly remind the students to use the discussion prompts they learned when they participate in class discussions. The prompts are:

* "I agree with _____ because…"
* "I disagree with _____ because…"
* "In addition to what _____ said, I think…"

Teacher Note

If the students have difficulty answering this question, suggest some ideas like those in the "Students might say" note.

Students might say:

"If something is happening that you don't like, you could write a persuasive essay about it and send it to the newspaper. If other people read it, they might agree with you."

"I agree with [Sandeep]. You might write a persuasive essay to try to convince other people to agree with you."

"You might want to send a persuasive essay to the president or someone in the government to tell them about something that you think should be changed."

Explain that during writing time today the students may begin thinking about topics they might want to write a persuasive essay about, or they may write about anything else they choose.

WRITING TIME

Write Independently

Ask the students to return to their seats for 20–30 minutes of silent writing. During this time, they may list topics they might want to write a persuasive essay about or write about anything they choose.

If necessary, remind the students that all writing should be double-spaced and that there should be no talking, whispering, or walking around during the silent writing period. Join the students in writing for a few minutes; then walk around the room and observe.

Signal to let the students know when writing time is over.

Teacher Note

Note that on Days 1 and 2 of this week, the students may do persuasive writing or write about anything else they choose. On Day 3, after exposure to more examples of persuasive writing, all the students will be asked to begin writing in this genre.

SHARING AND REFLECTING

Briefly Share Writing and Reflect

Ask partners to talk briefly about what they wrote today. Alert the students to be ready to share their partner's ideas with the class. After a moment, signal for their attention and ask:

Q *What did your partner write about today?*

Q *What did you and your new partner do to work well together when you were talking and sharing your writing?*

Day 2

Materials

- "Television: The Most Disparaged Resource of the Information Age" (see page 501)
- *Student Writing Handbook* pages 27–29
- Chart paper and a marker

Exploring Persuasive Writing

In this lesson, the students:

- Hear and discuss a persuasive essay
- Think about the author's audience and purpose
- Generate possible opinions for persuasive essays
- Write about things that interest them

GETTING READY TO WRITE

1 ▶ **Discuss Audience**

Gather the class with partners sitting together, facing you. Ask them to bring their *Student Writing Handbooks* with them.

Review that yesterday the students read a persuasive essay called "WARNING: Too Much TV Is Hazardous to Your Health." Ask:

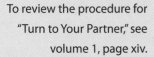

Q *What do you remember about what the author is trying to do in this essay? Turn to your partner.*

Teacher Note ▶

To review the procedure for "Turn to Your Partner," see volume 1, page xiv.

Have partners discuss their thinking; then have a few volunteers share with the class. Ask the students to open to *Student Writing Handbook* pages 27–28 and briefly review the essay. Ask:

Q *What kind of person do you think this author is writing to, and why?*

Teacher Note ▶

If the students have difficulty answering this question, suggest some ideas like those in the "Students might say" note.

Students might say:

"I think this author is writing to people who watch too much TV. It's all about how bad it is for you."

"In addition to what [Blanca] said, I think the author is writing to parents of kids. I think so because in the first paragraph it says 'our kids.'"

Point out that, while many different kinds of people are likely to read a persuasive essay, authors of persuasive essays usually have a certain kind of reader (or *audience*) in mind when they are writing. In this case, the reader is likely to be a person who watches a lot of TV or whose family watches a lot of TV.

Explain that the students will hear and read another persuasive essay today. Encourage them to think about who the audience for this essay might be.

Read "Television: The Most Disparaged Resource of the Information Age" Aloud

Have the students open to *Student Writing Handbook* page 29, where today's essay, "Television: The Most Disparaged Resource of the Information Age," is reproduced. Invite them to follow along as you read the essay aloud. Explain that *disparaged* means "ridiculed or spoken badly about." This essay is written by a teenager named Salmaan S.

Read the essay aloud slowly and clearly. Clarify vocabulary as you read.

Suggested Vocabulary

audio-visual stimuli: things you can hear and see

most efficient means of mass communication: best ways to communicate with lots of people

Tiananmen Square incident: a violent incident in China that appeared in the news

fall of the Berlin Wall: an important world event that appeared in the news

Vietnam: short for the Vietnam War

appliance: machine

ELL Vocabulary

English Language Learners may benefit from discussing additional vocabulary, including:

transfer thoughts and ideas: tell other people thoughts and ideas

other cultures: other kinds of people

unites: brings together

enormous: huge

3▸ **Briefly Discuss the Author's Audience and Purpose**

In pairs and as a class, briefly discuss:

 Q *What is Salmaan S. trying to convince us of in this essay? Turn to your partner.*

Students might say:

"He's trying to convince us that watching TV is not a waste of time."

"He's saying that TV is important because it brings people together."

Point out that the persuasive essay they read yesterday tried to convince them of the opposite point of view. Ask and briefly discuss:

Q *Who do you think Salmaan is writing to (or, who is the audience)?*

Q *In the sentence, "Well, I strongly disagree with the viewpoint that television is a waste of time," Salmaan tells us exactly what his opinion is. He then gives us several reasons that support his opinion. What reasons does he give?*

Q *Compare this essay to the one you read yesterday. Which essay is more persuasive to you, and why?*

Students might say:

"I think the audience might be people who think TV is a waste of time. Otherwise why would he be trying to convince them?"

"I agree with [Ricardo]. One reason he gives to support his opinion is that it's one of the quickest ways to present an idea clearly."

"I think yesterday's essay is more persuasive. It gives reasons for why TV is bad for your health."

"I disagree with [Lars]. Today's essay is more convincing because it makes me realize how much we learn from watching TV."

4▸ **Generate Possible Opinions for Persuasive Essays**

Explain that people often write persuasive essays when they have strong opinions about whether something is good or bad, right or wrong. In the two essays they have read so far, one author feels that television is a good thing, while the other feels that too much TV can be harmful. On a sheet of chart paper entitled "Possible

Teacher Note ▸

If students have difficulty answering these questions, suggest some ideas like those in the "Students might say" note.

Opinions for Persuasive Essays," write the sentences *Television is good* and *Too much TV is harmful*.

Ask the students to watch as you write a few other opinions on the chart. Add a few sentences that reflect opinions that you hold.

Possible Opinions for Persuasive Essays

Television is good.

Too much TV is harmful.

Jazz is the best kind of music.

High-heeled shoes are bad for your feet.

Donuts are not a healthy breakfast food.

It's wrong to say mean things to people.

Use "Think, Pair, Share" to have partners first think about and then discuss:

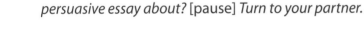

Q *What opinions do you have that you might be able to write a persuasive essay about?* [pause] *Turn to your partner.*

Students might say:

"It's not right to exclude people."

"Hip-hop is the best kind of music."

"I have a strong opinion that lima beans are gross."

"Smoking is hazardous to your health."

"I think bullying is wrong."

As the students report ideas, record them on the chart. Tell them that you will add to the chart as they think of more ideas in the coming days.

Explain that today the students may continue to think about topics for persuasive essays, write about some of their opinions, or write about anything they choose.

◀ **Teacher Note**

To review the procedure for "Think, Pair, Share," see volume 1, page xiv.

WRITING TIME

 ## Write Independently

Ask the students to return to their seats. Write the following choices on the board and have them write silently for 20–30 minutes.

- Think about topics you might want to write a persuasive essay about.

- Write about your opinions.

- Write about anything you choose.

Join the students in writing for a few minutes; then walk around the room and observe.

Signal to let the students know when quiet writing time is over.

SHARING AND REFLECTING

 ## Briefly Share Writing and Reflect

Ask partners to talk briefly about what they wrote today. Alert the students to be ready to share their partner's ideas with the class. After a moment, signal for their attention and ask:

Q *What did your partner write about today?*

Q *What did you and your new partner do to work well together when you were talking and sharing your writing?*

Teacher Note

Save the "Possible Opinions for Persuasive Essays" chart to use on Day 3 and later in the unit.

Day 3

Exploring Persuasive Writing

In this lesson, the students:

- Hear, discuss, and write persuasive essays
- Think about features of persuasive essays
- Think about the author's audience and purpose
- Quick-write about their opinions

GETTING READY TO WRITE

▶ Review Persuasive Essays

Gather the class with partners sitting together, facing you. Ask the students to bring their *Student Writing Handbooks*, notebooks, and pencils with them. Review that they read two persuasive essays earlier this week on the topic of television. Ask them to open to *Student Writing Handbook* pages 27–29 and briefly review the essays. Ask:

Q *What were the authors of these two essays trying to do?*

Q *What do the authors do in these essays to try to convince us of their points of view?*

As the students respond, record their ideas on a sheet of chart paper entitled "Things We Notice About Persuasive Essays." If necessary, point out that the authors clearly state their opinions early in the essay, and then follow their opinions with several examples to support them. Add *author clearly states opinion early in the piece* and *author gives reasons that support the opinion* to the chart if similar ideas are not already recorded.

Explain that today the students will hear and read another persuasive essay, this one on a different topic. Invite them to think about what else they notice the author doing as they read.

Materials

- "Animal Experimentation Saves Lives" (see page 502)
- "Possible Opinions for Persuasive Essays" chart from Day 2
- Chart paper and a marker
- *Student Writing Handbook* pages 27–31
- *Assessment Resource Book*

FACILITATION TIP

During this unit, we encourage you to **avoid repeating or paraphrasing** students' responses. It is easy to habitually repeat what students say when they speak too softly, or to paraphrase them when they don't speak clearly. Doing this teaches students to listen to you but not necessarily to one another. Try refraining from repeating or paraphrasing and see what happens. Encourage the students to take responsibility by asking one another to speak up or by asking a question if they don't understand what a classmate has said. (See the front matter for special considerations for English Language Learners.)

Read "Animal Experimentation Saves Lives" Aloud

Have the students open to *Student Writing Handbook* pages 30–31, where today's essay, "Animal Experimentation Saves Lives," is reproduced. Explain that "animal experimentation" refers to using animals in science experiments to learn about human diseases and to develop medicines and other products for human use. Often these animals feel pain and die as a result of these experiments. Point out that animal experimentation is an example of a topic that many people have strong opinions about.

Invite the students to follow along as you read the essay aloud. Read it aloud slowly and clearly, clarifying vocabulary as you read.

> **Suggested Vocabulary**
>
> **vaccines:** medicines that prevent disease
>
> **polio epidemic crippled and killed children:** many, many children were crippled and killed by a disease called polio
>
> **sacrifice:** kill for a reason
>
> **priorities:** what's important
>
> **with a fast reproduction rate:** that have a lot of babies quickly
>
> **ELL Vocabulary**
>
> English Language Learners may benefit from discussing additional vocabulary, including:
>
> **it may not be common knowledge:** people may not know this
>
> **diabetes, cancer, AIDS/HIV:** names of diseases
>
> **claiming thousands of lives:** killing thousands of people
>
> **rodents:** the family of animals that includes rats and mice

 Briefly Discuss the Author's Audience and Purpose

Ask and briefly discuss:

Q *What is Giovanny P. trying to convince us of?*

Q *Who do you think Giovanny is writing to (or who is the audience)?*

Q *In the sentence, "The use of animal experimentation should be recognized and accepted as a tool in saving lives," the author tells*

Teacher Note ▶

If students have difficulty answering these questions, suggest some ideas like those in the "Students might say" note.

us exactly what his opinion is. He gives us several reasons for his opinion. What reasons does he give?

Students might say:

"He's trying to convince us that it's okay to experiment on animals because it benefits everyone."

"I agree with [Gwen]. I think the audience might be people who disagree with animal experimentation."

"In addition to what [Richard] said, he gives examples of how animal experimentation cured polio and rabies."

Quick-Write: Opinions

Direct the students' attention to the "Possible Opinions for Persuasive Essays" chart and review the items on it. Explain that the students will choose one topic on the chart that they have some opinions about and do a 5-minute quick-write about it. Ask the students to watch as you model doing a quick-write about your opinions.

Think aloud about a topic on the chart that you can write about; then model writing a sentence stating that opinion followed by some reasons that support it.

When you finish writing, point out how you stated your opinion clearly and then wrote a couple of reasons that support your opinion.

Use "Think, Pair, Share" to have partners first think about and then discuss:

Q *What opinion on the chart will you choose, and what will you write?* [pause] *Turn to your partner.*

After partners have talked, ask the students to open to the next blank page of their writing notebooks and to write for 5 minutes.

When time is up, signal for the students' attention and have a few volunteers share what they wrote with the class. Explain that during writing time today you would like all the students to write about their opinions. They may continue the piece they started during the quick-write, or they may start a new piece and write about any opinions they feel strongly about.

◀ **Teacher Note**

You might write, *Donuts are not a healthy breakfast food. They are full of sugar and fat. They give you energy for a short time and then leave you feeling tired and hungry again long before lunch. Oatmeal is a healthier choice because it has less sugar and fat and will give you energy all morning.*

WRITING TIME

 Write Independently

Ask the students to return to their seats. Write the following choices on the board and have them write silently for 20–30 minutes.

* Continue the piece you started during the quick-write.

* Start a new piece about an opinion you have.

Join the students in writing for a few minutes; then walk around the room and observe.

CLASS ASSESSMENT NOTE

Observe the students and ask yourself:

* Are the students able to identify opinions to write about?

* Can they state their opinions clearly in their writing?

* Can they give reasons that support their opinions?

If you notice many students struggling to write after 10–15 minutes, call for the class's attention and have a few volunteers share what they have written so far; then have the students resume writing on their own for a few more minutes.

Record your observations in the *Assessment Resource Book*.

Signal to let the students know when writing time is over.

SHARING AND REFLECTING

 Briefly Share Writing and Reflect

Ask and briefly discuss:

Q *What opinion did you write about today?*

Q   *Did you state your opinion clearly in one sentence? Read it to us.*

Q   *What reasons did you give for your opinion? Read one of them to us.*

Explain that the students will continue to write about their opinions tomorrow.

Teacher Note

Save the "Possible Opinions for Persuasive Essays" and the "Things We Notice About Persuasive Essays" charts to use on Day 4.

Day 4

Materials

- "Animal Testing: Here Is the Truth" (see page 503)
- "Things We Notice About Persuasive Essays" chart from Day 3
- "Possible Opinions for Persuasive Essays" chart
- *Student Writing Handbook* pages 30–32
- *Assessment Resource Book*

Exploring Persuasive Writing

In this lesson, the students:

- Hear and discuss a persuasive essay
- Think about the author's audience and purpose
- Write about their opinions
- Respectfully consider the opinions of others

GETTING READY TO WRITE

1 Gather and Review Persuasive Essays

Gather the class with partners sitting together, facing you. Ask the students to bring their *Student Writing Handbooks* with them. Review that they read a persuasive essay about animal experimentation yesterday. Ask them to open their *Student Writing Handbooks* to pages 30–31 and quickly review the essay. Ask and briefly discuss:

Q *What opinion does the author of this essay have about animal experimentation?*

Direct the students' attention to the "Things We Notice About Persuasive Essays" chart, and review that in persuasive essays, authors clearly state an opinion early in the piece and then follow this with reasons that support the opinion. Explain that today the students will hear and read another persuasive essay about animal experimentation, this one with a different point of view. Invite them to think about what the author's opinion is in this essay.

2 Read "Animal Testing: Here Is the Truth" Aloud

Have the students open to *Student Writing Handbook* page 32, where today's essay, "Animal Testing: Here Is the Truth," is reproduced. Invite them to follow along as you read the essay aloud.

Read the essay aloud slowly and clearly, clarifying vocabulary as you read.

Suggested Vocabulary

detergents: soaps

cosmetics: make-up

side effects: unexpected, harmful results such as an allergic reaction

advantageous: good for, beneficial

solutions: liquid chemicals

cloned human cells: human cells made in a laboratory

Food and Drug Administration: government department responsible for the safety of food, medicine, and other products

ELL Vocabulary

English Language Learners may benefit from discussing additional vocabulary, including:

blinded: made unable to see

alternatives: other ideas or ways

3 ▶ Discuss Author's Audience and Purpose

In pairs and as a class, discuss:

Q *What sentences early in the essay tell us exactly what this author's opinion is about animal testing?*

Q *What are some reasons she gives to support her opinion that animal testing is cruel and unnecessary? Turn to your partner.*

Q *Who do you think Emma is writing to (or, who is the audience)? Turn to your partner.*

Students might say:

"The sentences 'Even though animal testing is advantageous to humans, I believe humankind should not test products on animals. It is cruel and unnecessary' tells us what her opinion is."

"I agree with [Taro]. One reason she gives is the horrible tests that make the animals suffer and die."

"In addition to what [Karen] said, the author says scientists have alternatives to animal testing."

"I think the audience is people who think animal testing is okay. She's trying to convince them that it's not."

◀ **Teacher Note**

If students have difficulty answering these questions, suggest some ideas like those in the "Students might say" note.

Add to "Possible Opinions for Persuasive Essays" Chart

Direct the students' attention to the "Possible Opinions for Persuasive Essays" chart and review the items on it. Remind the students that the two essays they read about animal testing had opposing opinions. Add the sentences *Animal testing is right* and *Animal testing is wrong* to the chart. Ask:

Q *What other opinions do you have that you might be able to write a persuasive essay about?*

Add any suggestions to the chart. Explain that during writing time today, all of the students will write about opinions they have. They may continue the piece they started yesterday, or they may start a new piece using the charted opinions or any other opinions they have. Refer to the "Things We Notice About Persuasive Essays" chart and remind the students to clearly state their opinion early in the piece and to give reasons that support their opinions.

WRITING TIME

 Write Independently

Ask the students to return to their seats. Write the following choices on the board and have them write silently for 20–30 minutes.

● Continue the essay that you started yesterday.

● Start a new essay about an opinion you have.

Join the students in writing for a few minutes; then walk around the room and observe.

CLASS ASSESSMENT NOTE

Continue to observe the students and ask yourself:

- Are the students able to identify opinions to write about?
- Can they state their opinions clearly in their writing?
- Can they give reasons that support their opinions?

If you notice many students struggling to write after 10–15 minutes, call for the class's attention and have a few volunteers share what they have written so far; then have the students resume writing on their own for a few more minutes.

Record your observations in the *Assessment Resource Book*.

Signal to let the students know when writing time is over.

SHARING AND REFLECTING

Briefly Share Writing and Discuss Disagreeing Respectfully

Ask partners to share what they wrote with each other. Alert the students to be ready to share their partner's ideas with the class. After a few moments, signal for attention and ask:

Q *What opinion did your partner write about today?*

Q *Do you have the same opinion as your partner or a different opinion? Explain.*

Explain that in the coming week, the students will develop a persuasive essay on a topic they feel strongly about. They will share their opinions with their partner and with the whole class, and they may sometimes disagree or have opposing opinions. Ask:

Q *Why is it important that we find a respectful way to talk to one another about our opinions, especially if we disagree?*

Teacher Note

Save the "Possible Opinions for Persuasive Essays" and the "Things We Notice About Persuasive Essays" charts to use in Week 2.

Students might say:

"It's important to talk about our opinions because that's how we learn from each other."

"It's important to be respectful because everyone is allowed to have their own opinion."

"It's okay if we disagree. We're not all going to think the same thing all the time."

Explain that the students will explore ways to talk about their opinions in a respectful way in the coming weeks.

EXTENSION

Read Editorials and Letters to the Editor

Collect newspapers and magazines that have op-ed pieces or letters to the editor that might be accessible for your students. Read these together as a class or make them available for the students to read independently. Take time to discuss what the author's opinion is, how that opinion is supported in the piece, and whether the students are persuaded by the piece.

WARNING: Too Much TV Is Hazardous to Your Health

(adapted from www.tvturnoff.org)

More than four hours a day: that's how much television Americans watch on average. As an abundance of evidence makes clear, our television habit has serious negative consequences. Excessive TV-watching cuts into family time, harms our kids' ability to read and perform well in school, encourages violence, and promotes sedentary lifestyles and obesity.

TV Undermines Family Time

Many people feel that they do not have enough time to spend with their families…television plays a crucial role. In the average American household, the TV is on for 7 hours, 40 minutes a day, and 40 percent of Americans report always or often watching television while eating dinner. Families who watch little or no television often find that they have more time to spend with one another.

TV Harms Reading and Academic Performance

Excessive television-watching harms reading skills…researcher[s] [found] more than a decade ago that "reading scores diminished sharply for those students watching more than four hours a day." Researchers such as Jane Healy of Harvard argue that watching TV instead of reading may actually [change] the physical structure of the brain as it develops, making learning and working in the schoolroom environment difficult.

TV Encourages Violence

The evidence is overwhelming: violence on TV promotes violent behavior in real life. Of more than 3,500 research studies on the effects of media violence over the past 40 years, 99.5 percent have shown a positive correlation between watching violence on TV and committing acts of real-life violence.

continues

WARNING: Too Much TV Is Hazardous to Your Health
continued

TV Promotes Sedentary Lifestyles and Obesity

Americans, by and large, do not get enough physical exercise. We spend most of our free time watching television, which promotes obesity and its related illnesses. According to Dr. William Dietz at the Centers for Disease Control, "The easiest way to reduce inactivity is to turn off the TV set. Almost anything else uses more energy than watching TV."

Essay

Television: The Most Disparaged Resource of the Information Age

by Salmaan S., Westford, MA

(adapted from www.teenink.com)

Almost every day one can hear some mention of "The TV generation of the '90s." Many harshly label television as a "drug," claiming that millions of children every day waste their time in front of this electronic altar. Well, I strongly disagree with the viewpoint that television is a waste of time.

Today, there are many different ways to transfer thoughts and ideas. Of these, television, with its combination of audio-visual stimuli, is one of the quickest to present an idea clearly and completely. To say that television is not important is to say that learning about other cultures thousands of miles away by seeing and hearing is a waste of time. In this age of information, television is one of the most efficient means of mass communication available to man.

Where else could billions of people have [seen] the horrors of the Tiananmen Square incident or witnessed firsthand man's first steps on the moon? In what other way could people have simultaneously experienced the fall of the Berlin Wall or Vietnam?

Television unites mankind because people separated by distance, skin color, language and wealth can all relate to some of the things they see on TV. No other appliance of the information age is as quick and widely used around the world as television. Failing to acknowledge the positive value of this resource to mankind is an enormous mistake.

Animal Experimentation Saves Lives
by Giovanny P., San Gabriel, CA
(adapted from www.teenink.com)

It may not be common knowledge, but animals save lives each and every day. Animal experimentation has existed since ancient times to contribute to human life and survival. These experiments became the building blocks of health and medicine, [including] research of diabetes, vaccines, cancer, AIDS/HIV and open-heart surgery. As a result, many people have been saved. The use of animal experimentation should be recognized and accepted as a tool in saving lives.

In the 1940s and 1950s, a polio epidemic crippled and killed children and newborns. Without animal experimentation [to develop a polio vaccine], polio would still be claiming thousands of lives each year. Many would not be alive today without it.

Louis Pasteur, a French chemist, helped save animals as well as humans when he developed a vaccine for rabies [using animal experimentation]. Today, animal-lovers everywhere do not have to put their pets "to sleep" if they [catch] rabies. Instead they can just go to their veterinarian and get this preventive vaccine.

"Nobody I know of in biological research, who has to sacrifice animals, likes it," says Richard Jones, a biology professor at Colorado University. "It is a matter of priorities. You work for the greater good." [Millions of] animals are used [in experiments], of which 90% are rodents. So it's not as if scientists experiment on endangered species; they use animals with a fast reproduction rate that are abundant.

Humans have vast intelligence, and through this intelligence, they have a moral duty: to protect all living things and make sure they survive and flourish. Animal experimentation helps humans help themselves, as well as the animals around them.

Essay

Animal Testing: Here Is the Truth

by Emma H., New York, NY

(adapted from www.teenink.com)

Almost every major company that sells detergents, body washes, or cosmetics tests their products on animals to assure the public that there will be no side effects when using their product. Even though animal testing is advantageous to humans, I believe humankind should not test products on animals. [It] is cruel and unnecessary.

Every year thousands of animals are killed, tortured, or left with burns, broken bones, and other terrible conditions. According to the National Anti-Vivisection Society, these are some of the most common yet horrifying tests used on animals: in the D test solutions are dropped directly into the eyes of rabbits and in seven days of testing, the rabbits experience excruciating pain and most are blinded. Then there is the LD-50 test [which forces animals to inhale, swallow, and digest chemicals]. In this test 50% of the animals die.

What will scientists test products on if not animals? With modern technology, many alternatives have been found by caring scientists [including computer tests and tests on cloned human cells]. These are only a few of the alternatives, but they show that animals are not the only choice for experimentation.

The Food and Drug Administration [urges] companies to conduct tests to ensure the safety of their products. As a result, animals continue to be the victims of harsh treatment and risk death. There are many alternatives to know if a product is safe. Animal testing is immoral and wrong.

GENRE: PERSUASIVE NONFICTION

Essay

"School Uniforms"
adapted from essay by Akinyi R. on www.teenink.com
(see page 525)

School uniforms eliminate distractions in school, create a less
judgmental environment, and save time and money.

Writing Focus

- Students hear and discuss persuasive essays.

- Students choose a topic and write a persuasive essay about it.

- Students state an opinion and use examples to support it.

- Students check for accuracy.

- Students explore strong openings and conclusions for persuasive essays.

Social Focus

- Students listen to the thinking of others and share their own.

- Students express interest in and appreciation for one another's writing.

- Students act in fair and caring ways.

TEACHER AS WRITER

"I'm still doing business at the same old stand—love, work, war, death, what the world is like outside this window tonight."
                 — Alan Dugan

Look at the list of things that "bug" you that you wrote in Week 1. Select an item on the list and write a paragraph expressing your opinion about how this thing should be changed. Do this for several other items on the list that you feel strongly about.

Day 1

Materials

- "School Uniforms" (see page 525)
- "Possible Opinions for Persuasive Essays" chart from Week 1
- "Things We Notice About Persuasive Essays" chart from Week 1
- *Student Writing Handbook* pages 33–34
- "Conference Notes" record sheet for each student (BLM1)

Exploring Persuasive Writing

In this lesson, the students:

- Hear, discuss, and write a persuasive essay
- Think about the author's audience and purpose
- Choose an opinion and audience for a persuasive essay
- Respectfully consider the opinions of others
- Agree and disagree in a caring way

GETTING READY TO WRITE

 Briefly Review Persuasive Essays

Gather the class with partners sitting together, facing you. Ask them to bring their *Student Writing Handbooks* with them. Remind them that last week they began exploring persuasive essays. They read four persuasive essays—two about TV viewing and two about animal experimentation. Ask:

Q *What did you learn last week about persuasive essays?*

Briefly review the "Things We Notice About Persuasive Essays" chart and add any new ideas to the chart. Remind the students that they brainstormed opinions that they might want to write a persuasive essay about. Review the items on the "Possible Opinions for Persuasive Essays" chart.

 Discuss Expressing Personal Opinions

Explain that each of the authors of last week's essays expressed their opinions, even though they knew some people would probably disagree with them. Ask and briefly discuss:

Q *What might be hard about expressing an opinion that you know other people might disagree with?*

Q *If you really believe something, why is it important to express that opinion even though others might not agree with you?*

Students might say:

"It might be hard to express an opinion because people might say you're stupid."

"It might be embarrassing if no one else agrees with you."

"It's important to express your opinion because people need to think for themselves."

"I agree with [Akeisha]. Plus everyone else might be wrong. Martin Luther King, Jr. kept expressing his opinion even though lots of people didn't agree with him, but he was right."

Tell the students that they will read and discuss another persuasive essay today, and then they will begin writing persuasive essays on a topic that is important to them. Tell them that it is important for everyone in the class to feel safe and comfortable expressing their opinions, both in speaking and in writing. Ask:

Q *What can you do when listening to other people's opinions to make it safe and comfortable for everyone?*

Q *What can you do when expressing your own opinions to make it safe and comfortable for everyone?*

Students might say:

"When I'm listening to someone else, I can try to see things from that person's point of view."

"In addition to what [Phillip] said, if I disagree with someone, I can use our prompt, 'I disagree with him because….'"

"When I'm expressing my opinion, I can remember that everyone might not agree with me."

"In addition to what [Rhonda] said, maybe I'll change my mind when I hear someone else's opinion."

Encourage the students to keep in mind the things they talked about and tell them that you will check in with them to see how they did.

◀ **Teacher Note**

If the students have difficulty answering this question, suggest some ideas like those in the "Students might say" note.

3 Read "School Uniforms" Aloud

Have the students open to *Student Writing Handbook* pages 33–34, where today's essay, "School Uniforms," is reproduced. Invite them to follow along as you read the essay aloud.

Read the essay aloud slowly and clearly, clarifying vocabulary as you read.

> **Suggested Vocabulary**
>
> **eliminate:** take away
>
> **parochial school:** private school connected with a church
>
> **economic advantages and disadvantages:** wealth or lack of wealth (poverty)

> **ELL Vocabulary**
>
> English Language Learners may benefit from discussing additional vocabulary, including:
>
> **were no longer obvious:** could not be seen anymore
>
> **impress:** show off to

4 Discuss the Author's Purpose

In pairs and as a class, discuss:

Q *What is Akinyi trying to convince us about in this essay?*

Q *What are some reasons Akinyi gives to support the opinion that students should wear uniforms in public schools?*

 Q *Do you agree or disagree with the opinion in this essay, and why? Turn to your partner.*

Teacher Note ▶

If students have difficulty answering these questions, suggest some ideas like those in the "Students might say" note.

> **Students might say:**
>
> "I think the sentence 'I believe students in public school should be required to wear them' tells us pretty clearly what this author's opinion is."
>
> "One reason Akinyi gives to support her opinion is that it takes away the distractions of clothes so kids can focus on studying."
>
> "In addition to what [Daryl] said, it sounds like it saves time and money."

"I agree with the author. I think uniforms would make it so everyone is treated fairly."

"I disagree with the author. Wearing uniforms would make me feel like I was in the army."

▶ Select an Opinion and Audience for Their Persuasive Essay

Direct the students' attention to the "Possible Opinions for Persuasive Essays" chart and review the items on it. Add the sentences *Uniforms should be required in public school* and *Uniforms should not be required in public school* to the chart. Ask:

Q   *What other opinions for persuasive essays could we add to the chart?*

Add any suggestions to the chart. Explain that today the students will choose one opinion that they have not yet written about and begin writing a draft of a persuasive essay, double-spaced, in their notebooks. This week they will work on developing and revising their essays, and next week they will proofread and publish them. They will publish them for the class, as well as for readers outside the class, to read.

Write the following three questions where everyone can see them. Have the students think about these questions quietly for a few moments and then discuss their thinking about them in pairs.

- What opinion do you feel strongly enough about to publish a persuasive essay about it?
- In addition to your classmates, whom will you be trying to convince (who will be your audience)?
- What might you do to get a person from that audience to read your essay?

Teacher Note ▶

You might say, "[Jonas] says he wants to convince his mother that he should be allowed to play video games as much as he likes as long as he finishes his homework. While he's writing his essay, he's going to remember whom he's trying to convince."

After partners have talked, signal for their attention and have a few volunteers share their thinking with the class. As they report, emphasize that they should keep their audience in mind as they write today.

WRITING TIME

6 ▶ Write Independently

Ask the students to return to their seats and work on their persuasive essays for 20–30 minutes. Remind them to write their drafts double-spaced in their notebooks. Join them in writing for a few minutes; then begin conferring with individual students.

TEACHER CONFERENCE NOTE

Over the next two weeks, confer with individual students about their persuasive essay drafts. Have each student tell you about and read his draft as you ask yourself the following questions:

- Is this student able to identify an opinion to write about?

- Does he state his opinion clearly early in the piece?

- Does he give several different reasons that support his opinion?

Support students' thinking by asking them questions such as:

Q *What is the opinion you are writing about?*

Q *Whom are you trying to convince? What do you want to convince them of?*

Q *Why do you believe your opinion is correct? What other reasons can you give?*

Q *How can you state your opinion clearly at the beginning of your piece?*

Q *What reason will you write about first? Second? Third?*

Document your observations for each student using the "Conference Notes" record sheet (BLM1). Use the "Conference Notes" record sheets during conferences throughout this unit.

Signal to let the students know when writing time is over.

SHARING AND REFLECTING

7 ▶ Briefly Share Writing and Reflect

Ask partners to talk briefly about what they wrote today. After a moment, signal for their attention and ask:

Q *What opinion did your partner write about today? Whom is she trying to convince in her essay?*

Q *Do you and your partner agree or disagree with each other's opinions? Turn to your partner and talk about this.*

Q *What did your partner say to let you know that he respects your opinion?*

Explain that the students will continue to develop their persuasive essays tomorrow.

FACILITATION TIP

Continue to try to **avoid repeating or paraphrasing** students' responses. Help them learn to participate responsibly in class discussions by encouraging them to ask one another to speak up or to ask a question if they don't understand what a classmate has said. (See the front matter for special considerations for English Language Learners.)

Day 2

Materials

- Transparencies of "School Uniforms" (BLM22–BLM23)

- Transparencies of "WARNING: Too Much TV Is Hazardous to Your Health" (BLM24–BLM25)

- Transparencies of "Television: The Most Disparaged Resource of the Information Age" (BLM26–BLM27)

- "Things We Notice About Persuasive Essays" chart

- *Student Writing Handbook* pages 27–29, 33–34

- Overhead pen

Drafting Persuasive Essays

In this lesson, the students:

- Explore strong openings and clear statements of opinion in persuasive essays
- Draft persuasive essays
- Express interest in and appreciation for one another's writing

GETTING READY TO WRITE

1 Briefly Review

Have partners sit together at desks today. Briefly review that they each picked a topic and began writing a persuasive essay yesterday. Explain that in the next three days they will develop their essay and that you will help them focus on and strengthen different parts of it to make it as persuasive as possible.

Direct the students' attention to the "Things We Notice About Persuasive Essays" chart, and review that good persuasive essays have a clear statement of opinion early in the piece. Explain that today they will look at the opening sentences of several essays to see what the authors did to get the audience interested and to make their opinions clear.

2 Analyze Opening Sentences

Show the transparencies of "School Uniforms" on the overhead projector and have the students turn to the essay on *Student Writing Handbook* pages 33–34. Read the first paragraph aloud as they follow along, then ask:

Q *What sentence in this essay tells us exactly what the author's opinion is?*

Underline the sentence "Yes, and I believe students in public school should be required to wear them," and ask the students to do the same in their *Student Writing Handbook*. Point out that this author opens the essay with a question and then states the opinion by answering the question. Ask:

Q *Why might starting an essay with a question be a good way to get a reader's attention?*

Students might say:

"When we read a question, we might get curious about the answer."

"It's more interesting than just starting with 'I believe students in public school should be required to wear uniforms.'"

Q *If you wanted to start your essay with a question, and then state your opinion in the answer, what might you write? Turn to your partner.*

Have partners talk for a few moments; then signal for their attention and have a few volunteers share what their opening question and answer might be.

Students might say:

"My essay could start, 'What is the best kind of music to listen to? It's hip hop!'"

"I could write, 'Should the driving age be lowered? Yes, I think it should be lowered to 12 years old.'"

"My opening sentences could be 'What's the worst thing that could happen to you at recess? The worst thing would be to have a bully pick on you.'"

As you did with "School Uniforms," discuss the opening sentences of "WARNING: Too Much TV Is Hazardous to Your Health" and "Television: The Most Disparaged Resource of the Information Age," using transparencies of the essays and *Student Writing Handbook* pages 27–29. Point out that, in both cases, the authors open their essays with sentences that alert the reader to the topic and state their opinions clearly in the first paragraph.

▶ Analyze Opening Sentences of Their Own Essays

Have the students reread the drafts of their essays quietly to themselves. After a moment, ask them to think—again quietly to

◀ **Teacher Note**

The opinion sentences in these two essays are: "As an abundance of evidence makes clear, our television habit has serious negative consequences" and "Well, I strongly disagree with the viewpoint that television is a waste of time."

themselves—about the following questions as you ask them one at a time. Pause between each question to give the students time to think.

Q *Do you have an opening sentence or question that will get your audience interested in reading your essay? If so, how will it interest them? If not, what might you write?*

Q *Do you state your opinion clearly somewhere in the first paragraph? If not, where might you state it, and what could you write?*

Have partners turn and discuss what they thought about as they listened to your questions. After a few moments, signal for their attention and have a few volunteers share their thinking with the class.

4▶ Discuss Resources

Explain that during writing time today the students will continue to work on their persuasive essays, adding reasons that support their opinion. Explain that you would also like them to work on their opening sentences and make sure that they have stated their opinion clearly in the first paragraph. Tell them that each student will share his opening sentence aloud with the class at the end of the period.

Point out that some students might feel the need to do a little research to find facts to support their opinion. Invite them to look for information about their topics on the Internet or in the class or school library.

Teacher Note

Because the students are familiarizing themselves with the genre of persuasive essay for the first time in grade 5, they are not expected to do extensive research to find data and facts to support their opinions at this point. This unit lays the foundation for more extensive study of the persuasive essay in subsequent grades.

WRITING TIME

5▶ Write Independently

Write the following tasks on the board and have the students work silently on them for 20–30 minutes. If necessary, remind them to double-space their drafts.

- Work on your persuasive essay.

- Revise your opening sentences to get your reader interested.

- Make sure to state your opinion clearly in the first paragraph.

- Make sure to give reasons that support your opinion.

Join the students in writing for a few minutes; then confer with individual students.

TEACHER CONFERENCE NOTE

Continue conferring with individual students about their persuasive essay drafts. Have each student tell you about and read her draft as you ask yourself the following questions:

- Is this student able to identify an opinion to write about?

- Is she able to write an opening that gets the reader interested?

- Does she state her opinion clearly in the first paragraph?

- Does she give several different reasons that support her opinion?

Support students' thinking by asking them questions such as:

Q *What is the opinion you are writing about?*

Q *Whom are you trying to convince? What do you want to convince them of?*

Q *Why do you believe your opinion is correct? What other reasons can you give?*

Q *What [question/sentence] might you write as your opening to get your reader interested in the topic?*

Q *How can you state your opinion clearly at the beginning of your piece?*

Q *What reason will you write first? Second? Third?*

Document your observations for each student using the "Conference Notes" record sheet (BLM1).

Signal to let the students know when writing time is over.

SHARING AND REFLECTING

 Share Opening Sentences and Reflect

Explain that the students will each read their opening sentence aloud. Ask the class to listen carefully to one another's sentences and to think about which ones make them curious.

Go around the room and have the students each read their opening sentence aloud, without comment. When all have read, ask and briefly discuss:

Q *What sentences did you hear that made you curious?*

Explain that the students will continue to develop their persuasive essays tomorrow.

Day 3

Drafting Persuasive Essays

In this lesson, the students:

- Explore how authors give supporting reasons in persuasive essays
- Draft persuasive essays
- Express interest in and appreciation for one another's writing
- Respectfully consider the opinions of others
- Agree and disagree in a caring way

Materials

- Transparencies of "WARNING: Too Much TV Is Hazardous to Your Health" (BLM24–BLM25)
- Transparencies of "School Uniforms" (BLM22–23)
- "Things We Notice About Persuasive Essays" chart
- *Student Writing Handbook* pages 27–28, 33–34

GETTING READY TO WRITE

▶ Analyze Supporting Paragraphs of Essays

Have partners sit together at desks today. Direct their attention to the "Things We Notice About Persuasive Essays" chart and review that good persuasive essays have a clear statement of opinion, and they also give reasons that support the opinion. Explain that today the students will look more closely at how authors give supporting reasons and then they will think about how they can be more persuasive in how they give reasons in their own essays.

Show the transparency of the first page of "WARNING: Too Much TV Is Hazardous to Your Health" on the overhead projector and have the students turn to the essay on *Student Writing Handbook* pages 27–28. Remind them that they looked at the first few sentences yesterday to see how the author gets the audience interested and states a clear opinion. Explain that you will reread parts of the essay. Ask the students to follow along as they think about how the author has organized this essay.

Read the first paragraph aloud; then read the four paragraph headings. Point out that after stating the opinion in the first paragraph, the author lists the four main supporting reasons that will be discussed in more detail in the four paragraphs of the essay (namely, TV undermines family time, harms reading and school performance, encourages violence, and promotes sedentary lifestyles and obesity). Ask:

Q *Why might an author want to organize his essay in this way?*

> **Students might say:**
>
> "It helps you keep track of the reasons if the author lists them up front."
>
> "Maybe in case you don't have time to read the whole essay you can get the main reasons in the first paragraph."

Read the next two paragraphs aloud as the students follow along. Point out that each of the paragraphs gives more information about its heading, including information from other resources (such as quotes from scientists and results of research studies).

Repeat this procedure with the transparencies of "School Uniforms" and the essay on *Student Writing Handbook* pages 33–34. Point out that this essay is organized in a way similar to the previous one: After the statement of the opinion, the author lists the three main supporting reasons that will be discussed in more detail in their own paragraphs in the essay (namely, uniforms eliminate distractions, allow children to be judged on personality rather than style, and save time and money).

▶ 2 Analyze the Opening Paragraphs of Their Own Essays

Have the students reread the drafts of their essays quietly to themselves. After a moment, ask them to quietly think about the following questions as you ask them one at a time. Pause between each question to give the students time to think.

Q *What are your main supporting reasons for your opinion? How many are there?*

Q *Do you list any of your supporting reasons in your first paragraph? If you wanted to use this technique, what could you write?*

Q *What can you add to your essay to give more information about your supporting reasons?*

Have partners turn and discuss what they thought about as they listened to your questions. After a few moments, signal for their attention and have a few volunteers share their thinking with the class.

▶ Prepare to Write

Explain that during writing time today, the students will continue to work on their persuasive essays, giving reasons to support their opinions. Encourage them to refer back in their *Student Writing Handbooks* to the two essays they looked at today to help them organize their own essays.

WRITING TIME

▶ Write Independently

Have the students work quietly on their essays for 20–30 minutes. Join them in writing for a few minutes; then confer with individual students.

> ◀ **Teacher Note**
>
> It may be challenging for students in grade 5 to organize their own essays based on "School Uniforms" and "WARNING: Too Much TV Is Hazardous to Your Health." It is sufficient at this grade for the students to be able to state an opinion clearly in the first paragraph and to follow this with several supporting reasons, organized in paragraphs or in any way that makes sense.

TEACHER CONFERENCE NOTE

Continue conferring with individual students about their persuasive essay drafts. Have each student tell you about and read her draft as you ask yourself the following questions:

- Is this student able to identify an opinion to write about?

- Is she able to write an opening that gets the reader interested?

- Does she state her opinion clearly in the first paragraph?

- Does she give several different reasons that support her opinion?

Support students' thinking by asking them questions like:

Q *Why do you believe your opinion is correct? What other reasons can you give?*

continues

> **TEACHER CONFERENCE NOTE** *continued*
>
> **Q** *How can you revise your opening to get your reader interested in the topic?*
>
> **Q** *How can you state your opinion clearly in the first paragraph?*
>
> **Q** *What other information can you give about your first reason?*
>
> Document your observations for each student using the "Conference Notes" record sheet (BLM1).

Signal to let the students know when writing time is over.

SHARING AND REFLECTING

 Share Opinion Statements and Reflect

Explain that each student will read one sentence from their essay that they feel is especially persuasive. Ask the students to listen carefully to their classmates' sentences and to think about whether they agree or disagree with the opinions.

Go around the room and have the students each read their sentences aloud, without comment. When all the students have read their sentences, ask and briefly discuss:

Q *What sentences did you hear that made you curious?*

Q *What sentences did you hear that you agree with? Why? That you disagree with? Why?*

Q *How are we doing with respectfully listening to and talking about our opinions? What can we do better?*

Explain that the students will finish drafting their persuasive essays tomorrow.

Day 4

Drafting Persuasive Essays

In this lesson, the students:

- Explore how authors conclude persuasive essays
- Finish drafting persuasive essays
- Express interest in and appreciation for one another's writing

Materials

- *Student Writing Handbooks* pages 27–29, 33–34
- "Things We Notice About Persuasive Essays" chart

GETTING READY TO WRITE

1 ▶ Analyze Conclusions of Essays

Have partners sit together at desks today. Remind them that in the past two days they explored how authors begin persuasive essays, clearly state opinions, and give reasons that support their opinions. Explain that today the students will look at how authors conclude, or end, their essays, and then they will think about how they want to conclude their own essays.

Ask partners to review the essays on *Student Writing Handbook* pages 27–29 and 33–34, focusing on the last sentence of each essay. Encourage them to think about what the author is doing in the last sentence. After a few moments, signal for their attention and ask:

Q *What do you notice about the last sentences of some of these essays?*

> **Students might say:**
>
> "In most of the essays, the author says his opinion again."
>
> "I agree with [Margaret]. The only essay where that doesn't happen is the one about TV being hazardous to your health."

If necessary, point out that in most cases the author restates his or her opinion at the end of the essay. Direct the students' attention to the "Things We Notice About Persuasive Essays" chart and add *author restates opinion at the end* to it.

Have the students review the drafts of their own essays for a few moments; then use "Think, Pair, Share" to have partners first think about and then discuss:

 Q *What might you write to restate your opinion at the end of your essay?* [pause] *Turn to your partner.*

After partners have discussed their thinking, signal for their attention and have a few volunteers share their thinking with the class.

2 ▶ Prepare to Write

On the "Things We Notice About Persuasive Essays" chart, use a marker to highlight the following three ideas:

* Author clearly states an opinion early in the piece.

* Author gives reasons that support the opinion.

* Author restates the opinion at the end.

Explain that during writing time today, the students will finish drafting their persuasive essays and get ready to proofread and publish them next week. When they believe they are finished, they should look at the highlighted items on the "Things We Notice About Persuasive Essays" chart and make sure they have included these things in their essay. They should also carefully reread their essay to make sure it makes sense.

WRITING TIME

3 ▶ Write Independently

Write the following tasks on the board and have the students write silently for 20–30 minutes.

* Finish writing your draft.

* Check the highlighted items on the "Things We Notice About Persuasive Essays" chart.

* Carefully reread your essay to make sure it makes sense.

Join the students in writing for a few minutes; then confer with individual students.

TEACHER CONFERENCE NOTE

Continue conferring with individual students about their persuasive essay drafts. Have each student tell you about and read his draft as you ask yourself the following questions:

- Is this student able to identify an opinion to write about?

- Is he able to write an opening that gets the reader interested?

- Does he state his opinion clearly in the first paragraph?

- Does he give several different reasons that support his opinion?

Support students' thinking by asking them questions like:

Q *Why do you believe your opinion is correct? What other reasons can you give?*

Q *How can you revise your opening to get your reader interested in the topic?*

Q *How can you state your opinion clearly in the first paragraph?*

Q *What other information can you give about your first reason?*

Document your observations for each student using the "Conference Notes" record sheet (BLM1).

Signal to let the students know when writing time is over.

SHARING AND REFLECTING

Share Concluding Sentences and Reflect

Explain that each student will read the last sentence of her essay aloud. Ask the students to listen carefully to one another and to think about whether they can tell what each person's essay is about from the last sentence.

Go around the room and have the students each read their last sentence aloud, without comment. When all have read, ask and briefly discuss:

Q *Could you tell what most of the essays are about from the last sentence? Why or why not?*

Q *What's interesting about hearing just single sentences of other people's writing?*

Explain that the students will proofread and publish their persuasive essays next week.

School Uniforms

by Akinyi R., Westford, MA

(adapted from www.teenink.com)

Are school uniforms appropriate for public school students? Yes, and I believe students in public school should be required to wear them. Uniforms eliminate the distractions of designer clothes so students can focus on their studies. Uniforms also create an environment in which children will be judged on personality rather than style. Finally, uniforms save time and money.

While attending a parochial school, I experienced the luxury of wearing uniforms. At my school, students came from diverse backgrounds. Inside the building, however, our economic advantages or disadvantages were no longer obvious. My friends and I were able to focus on academics and concern for others rather than the latest fashions. Since we looked similar, we remained attentive to the teacher and our work. I learned that my effort, attitude and aptitude were more important than my clothes.

Wearing uniforms helped me realize I don't need to impress anyone by the clothes I wear. School uniforms helped children who did not have "stylish" clothes to be treated fairly. I was judged by my character, not the price of my jeans. I had a chance to show my personality without worry that I was out of style. This set the tone in the school system that all individuals were to be treated as equals.

I never had to waste time deciding what to wear before school. A clean uniform was easy to maintain. My parents saved a lot of money, too. I did not need a variety of colors, styles and designer fashions in my wardrobe. Wearing uniforms helped me learn I did not always have to buy clothes I wanted when I wanted them.

When I wore a uniform, I started my day worry-free, focused on my schoolwork and felt judged by who I was on the inside. My family and I saved time and money. I believe children should be required to wear uniforms in public schools.

Week 3 Overview

GENRE: PERSUASIVE NONFICTION

Writing Focus

- Students confer about their persuasive essays.

- Students revise their essays based on partner feedback.

- Students explore the use of commas in direct quotations.

- Students proofread their essays for accuracy and correctness.

- Students publish their persuasive essays for the class and possibly for a wider audience.

Social Focus

- Students help one another improve their writing.

- Students express interest in and appreciation for one another's writing.

- Students listen respectfully to the thinking of others and share their own.

- Students make decisions and solve problems respectfully.

DO AHEAD

- (Optional) If computers are available, consider having some students type and print their essays. You might also recruit parent volunteers to help them.

TEACHER AS WRITER

"Look at what's happening in this world. Every day there's something exciting or disturbing to write about. With all that's going on, how could I stop?"
— *Gwendolyn Brooks*

Select one of the opinion paragraphs you wrote in Week 2 and develop it into a persuasive essay by listing several reasons that support your opinion. Devote a paragraph to each reason, providing information or rationale to justify your opinion. When you finish, consider having a friend or colleague read it and give you feedback about whether or not they are persuaded by your essay, and why.

Day 1

Materials

- Chart paper and a marker
- Supply of lined paper for final versions
- (Optional) Computers for word processing
- *Assessment Resource Book*

Pair Conferring and Revising

In this lesson, the students:

- Ask for and receive feedback about their writing
- Give feedback in a helpful way
- Ask one another questions about their writing
- Discuss and solve problems that arise in their work together

GETTING READY TO WRITE

 Prepare for Pair Conferences

Explain that today partners will meet to confer about their persuasive essay drafts. They will share their drafts and get feedback about anything confusing or unclear; then they will make any necessary revisions until they are convinced that their drafts make sense and are complete.

Remind the students that in the writing community the goal of giving feedback is to help each person create the best possible piece of writing. Ask and briefly discuss:

Q *What have you learned about giving feedback respectfully?*

Q *What problems can arise when giving feedback? How will you avoid those problems today?*

2 Prepare to Give Feedback: Does It All Make Sense?

Explain that, as partners listen to one another's writing, you would like them to ask themselves the three questions that follow. Write the questions on a sheet of chart paper labeled "Questions to Ask Myself as I Listen" as you say them aloud:

Questions to Ask Myself as I Listen

- Is it clear what this author's opinion is?

- Are there convincing reasons that support the opinion?

- Does this piece make sense? If not, where am I confused?

Encourage partners to ask themselves these questions and to listen carefully to each other. Explain that you would like the students to be ready to report the feedback they heard to the class.

Confer in Pairs

Give pairs ample time to confer.

CLASS ASSESSMENT NOTE

Circulate among conferring pairs and observe the conferences. Ask yourself:

- Are pairs staying on task, reading and discussing their writing?

- Are they giving each other specific feedback about the three charted questions?

- Are they giving feedback in a helpful and respectful way?

Make note of productive ways you see pairs interacting, as well as any problems, to bring up during Step 4.

Record your observations in the *Assessment Resource Book*.

When most pairs have had time to discuss their drafts, signal for the class's attention.

4 ▶ **Reflect on Feedback Received**

Ask and briefly discuss:

Q *What feedback did your partner give you that will help you revise your draft?*

Q *How was your partner respectful when giving you feedback?*

Q *I noticed that [partners were talking to each other in a kind way]. How did that [help/hinder] your work together?*

Explain that during writing time today, the students will revise their drafts based on their partner's feedback. If they finish, they may begin copying their draft neatly onto lined paper (or typing it on the computer) for their final version.

WRITING TIME

5 ▶ **Finish Revising Drafts and Begin Final Versions**

Have the students work on revising their drafts. Provide lined paper to students who finish revising and are ready to begin their final versions. As they work, circulate, observe, and offer assistance. When students seem to be working independently, confer with individual students.

TEACHER CONFERENCE NOTE

As you did in Week 2, confer with individual students about their persuasive essay drafts. Have each student tell you about and read his draft as you ask yourself the following questions:

- Is this student able to identify an opinion to write about?

- Is he able to write an opening that gets the reader interested?

- Does he state his opinion clearly in the first paragraph?

- Does he give several different reasons that support his opinion?

continues

TEACHER CONFERENCE NOTE *continued*

Support students' thinking by asking them questions such as:

Q *Why do you believe your opinion is correct? What other reasons can you give?*

Q *How can you revise your opening to get your reader interested in the topic?*

Q *How can you state your opinion clearly in the first paragraph?*

Q *What other information can you give about your first reason?*

Document your observations for each student using the "Conference Notes" record sheet (BLM1).

Signal to let the students know when writing time is over.

SHARING AND REFLECTING

6 ▶ Briefly Reflect on Writing

Help the students reflect on their work today by briefly discussing:

Q *Did you incorporate any of the feedback you received from your partner into your draft today? Read us the original passage and then read us the revision.*

Tell the students that they will proofread and finish writing their final versions tomorrow.

Day 2

Materials

- Transparencies of "Unpunctuated Passage from Persuasive Essay" (1 and 2) (BLM28–BLM29)

- Overhead pen

- *Student Writing Handbook* pages 27–28, 30–31, 35

- Supply of lined paper for final versions

- (Optional) Computers for word processing

Proofreading

In this lesson, the students:

- Practice punctuating text

- Listen for periods as they read their drafts aloud

- Explore using commas in direct quotations

- Proofread their drafts for spelling, punctuation, and grammar

- Work on their final versions for publication

GETTING READY TO WRITE

1 Prepare to Proofread

Have the students stay in their seats today. Explain that they will work on the final version of their persuasive essays. They will publish them by sharing them with the class from the Author's Chair later in the week and by placing them in the class library. They will also have the opportunity to publish them for readers outside the classroom, if they wish. Tell them that you will discuss this further with them later in the week.

Explain that the students will want to make their essays as clear as possible so nothing gets in the way of convincing their reader of their opinion. Today they will proofread their drafts to make sure they have corrected all errors before publishing.

2 Proofreading: Listening for Periods

As a class, practice listening for and punctuating the ends of sentences by showing the transparencies of the "Unpunctuated Passage from a Persuasive Essay" (1) and asking the students to follow along as you read it aloud. Read the passage without pauses and point out that right now the passage is one long sentence that doesn't sound right when read aloud.

Ask the students to slowly reread the passage with you and to stop when it feels natural to do so. At each stop (and as appropriate), model writing a comma or a period and capitalizing, where appropriate, to begin a new sentence. Also model capitalizing proper nouns and punctuating speech (including the correct use of commas in quotations). When finished, have the students check their punctuation against the original passage in the essay on *Student Writing Handbook* pages 30–31.

Have the students open their *Student Writing Handbook* to page 35 and read the next passage to themselves. Have them work in pairs to punctuate the passage, listening for the natural ends of sentences and capitalizing where appropriate. After a few moments, signal for their attention and have volunteers share how they punctuated the paragraph. Use the students' suggestions to punctuate the paragraph on the transparency. When finished, have the students check their punctuation against the original passage in the essay on *Student Writing Handbook* pages 27–28.

Explain that you would like the students to read their own drafts aloud today before beginning their final version to make sure they have used capital letters and periods, commas, quotation marks, and other punctuation as appropriate.

3 ▶ Briefly Review Proofreading with Word Bank and Proofreading Notes

Remind the students that, in addition to listening for the ends of sentences, they should use their word bank and proofreading notes to help them proofread their drafts for spelling errors and correctness before publishing (these components were introduced in Unit 2, Week 3, Days 1 and 2, on pages 128–135). Briefly review these procedures by reminding the students to:

- Circle words in their draft that they are unsure how to spell, and look them up in their word bank. They will add any words that are not already in their word bank after looking up their correct spelling in a dictionary or other source.

- Use their proofreading notes as a list of things to check in their draft before publishing. They will correct any errors by crossing out the error in their draft and writing the correction next to it.

◀ **Teacher Note**

To provide your students with more practice using commas in direct quotations and other capitalization and punctuation skills, do the related activities in the *Skill Practice Teaching Guide* with them.

◀ **Teacher Note**

If necessary, remind the students who have already begun writing their final version to correct any misspellings or errors they may have copied into their final version.

WRITING TIME

4▶ Proofread Drafts and Write Final Versions

Have the students work on proofreading their drafts. Provide lined paper to students who finish proofreading and are ready to begin their final versions. As they work, circulate, observe, and offer assistance. When students seem to be working independently, confer with individual students.

TEACHER CONFERENCE NOTE

Continue conferring with individual students about their persuasive essay drafts. Have each student tell you about and read his draft as you ask yourself the following questions:

* Is this student able to identify an opinion to write about?

* Is he able to write an opening that gets the reader interested?

* Does he state his opinion clearly in the first paragraph?

* Does he give several different reasons that support his opinion?

Support students' thinking by asking them questions like:

Q *Why do you believe your opinion is correct? What other reasons can you give?*

Q *How can you revise your opening to get your reader interested in the topic?*

Q *How can you state your opinion clearly in the first paragraph?*

Q *What other information can you give about your first reason?*

Document your observations for each student using the "Conference Notes" record sheet (BLM1).

Signal to let the students know when writing time is over.

SHARING AND REFLECTING

 Reflect on Proofreading

Ask and briefly discuss:

Q *What words did you find in your word bank today? How did you check on words that were not in the word bank?*

Q *What corrections did you make in your draft after reviewing your proofreading notes?*

Explain that the students will finish working on their final versions tomorrow.

Day 3

Materials

- Supply of lined paper for final versions
- (Optional) Computers for word processing
- Chair to use for Author's Chair sharing

Publishing

In this lesson, the students:

- Finish writing their final versions
- Present their essays from the Author's Chair
- Express interest in and appreciation for one another's writing
- Ask one another questions about their writing
- Respectfully consider the opinions of others

GETTING READY TO WRITE

 Briefly Review

Have the students stay in their seats today. Explain that they will finish working on the final version of their persuasive essays. Students who finish will begin sharing their pieces from the Author's Chair after the writing time.

Write the following tasks on the board and read them aloud:

- Finish proofreading your draft using your word bank and proofreading notes.
- Finish writing the final version of your persuasive essay.
- Reread it to make sure it is free of errors.
- If you finish, work on any other piece of writing.

Have the students think quietly to themselves for a moment about the following question:

Q *What do you need to work on today to be ready to share your persuasive essay from the Author's Chair?*

After a moment, have the students begin working independently.

WRITING TIME

2 Finish Final Versions of Persuasive Essays

Have the students work on finishing their final versions. When they seem to be working independently, confer with individual students.

TEACHER CONFERENCE NOTE

Continue conferring with individual students about their persuasive essay drafts. Have each student tell you about and read her draft as you ask yourself the following questions:

- Is this student able to identify an opinion to write about?

- Is she able to write an opening that gets the reader interested?

- Does she state her opinion clearly in the first paragraph?

- Does she give several different reasons that support her opinion?

Support students' thinking by asking them questions like:

Q *Why do you believe your opinion is correct? What other reasons can you give?*

Q *How can you revise your opening to get your reader interested in the topic?*

Q *How can you state your opinion clearly in the first paragraph?*

Q *What other information can you give about your first reason?*

Document your observations for each student using the "Conference Notes" record sheet (BLM1).

Signal to let the students know when writing time is over.

SHARING AND REFLECTING

 ### Review Sharing Writing from the Author's Chair

Gather the class with partners sitting together, facing the Author's Chair. Remind them of the procedure you have established for presenting writing from the Author's Chair.

Before asking a student to share from the Author's Chair today, discuss how the students will act, both as presenting authors and as members of the audience. Ask and discuss:

Q *How will you let the author know that you're interested in his or her piece? Why is it important to express interest in one another's writing?*

Q *How will you show that you respect the author's opinion, even if you disagree, and that you are carefully considering what he or she wrote?*

Remind the students that the purpose of the persuasive essay is to convince the reader of a particular opinion. Encourage them to think as they listen about whether they agree or disagree with the author's opinion and whether the essay is convincing them to change their mind.

 ### Conduct Author's Chair Sharing

Ask a student who has finished the final version of his persuasive essay to read it aloud from the Author's Chair. At the end of the sharing, facilitate a discussion using questions like those that follow, and give the author an opportunity to respond to the class's comments and questions:

Q *What did you learn about [smoking] from hearing [Vic's] essay?*

Q *Do you agree or disagree with his opinion? Why?*

Q *Were you persuaded to change your mind from hearing [Vic's] essay?*

Q *What questions can we ask [Vic] about what he wrote?*

Follow this procedure to have other students share from the Author's Chair.

5 ▶ Reflect on Audience Behavior During Author's Chair Sharing

Ask and briefly discuss:

Q *What did we do well as an audience today? What might we want to work on the next time authors share their work?*

Q *If you shared an essay today, did you feel that people were being respectful of your opinions and considering them carefully? Why or why not?*

Explain that all of the students will get a chance to share their essays from the Author's Chair in the coming days.

Teacher Note

As the students share their essays from the Author's Chair, collect them and compile them into a class book.

Day 4

Materials

- Supply of lined paper for final versions
- (Optional) Computers for word processing
- Chair to use for Author's Chair sharing

Publishing

In this lesson, the students:

- Discuss publishing for readers beyond the classroom
- Finish writing their final versions
- Present their essays from the Author's Chair
- Express interest in and appreciation for one another's writing
- Ask one another questions about their writing
- Respectfully consider the opinions of others

GETTING READY TO WRITE

▶1 Discuss Publishing Essays Beyond the Classroom

Gather the class with partners sitting together, facing you. Remind the students that the purpose of a persuasive essay is to convince the reader of a particular opinion. Ask, and have the students think quietly for a moment about:

Teacher Note ▶

If the students have difficulty answering this question, suggest some ideas like those in the "Students might say" note.

Q *Whom did you have in mind as the audience of your persuasive essay?*

Q *What do you want to convince them about?*

Q *What might you do to get a person from that audience to read your essay?*

After a moment, have a few volunteers share their thinking with the class.

Students might say:

"I wrote my essay for people who run factory farms so they
   can treat the animals better."

"I had the principal in my mind. I want to convince her to
   make lunchtime a full hour."

"I want my parents to read my essay. Maybe they will
   stop smoking."

"My essay is about putting more playgrounds in our
   neighborhood. I don't know who I would send my essay to."

"Maybe you could send it to our town's newspaper."

Some students may be interested in having someone from their
intended audience read their essay. Explain that these students
may do some extra research, with your help, to find out whom they
might send or give their essay to (see the Extension on page 544).

Remind the students that writers become better over time as they
practice writing over and over. Encourage students who feel drawn
to persuasive essays to continue to write them about opinions
they feel strongly about during their free time and during the open
weeks of this program.

Explain that the students will finish writing and publishing their final
versions today.

WRITING TIME

Finish Final Versions of Persuasive Essays

Have the students return to their seats and work on finishing
their persuasive essays. If they are finished, they may spend the
remaining time writing anything they choose. When they seem to
be working independently, confer with individual students.

TEACHER CONFERENCE NOTE

Continue conferring with individual students about their persuasive essay drafts. Have each student tell you about and read his draft as you ask yourself the following questions:

- Is this student able to identify an opinion to write about?

- Is he able to write an opening that gets the reader interested?

- Does he state his opinion clearly in the first paragraph?

- Does he give several different reasons that support his opinion?

Support students' thinking by asking them questions like:

Q *Why do you believe your opinion is correct? What other reasons can you give?*

Q *How can you revise your opening to get your reader interested in the topic?*

Q *How can you state your opinion clearly in the first paragraph?*

Q *What other information can you give about your first reason?*

Document your observations for each student using the "Conference Notes" record sheet (BLM1).

Signal to let the students know when writing time is over.

SHARING AND REFLECTING

 Gather for Author's Chair Sharing

Gather the class with partners sitting together, facing the Author's Chair. Remind the student of the procedure you established for presenting writing from the Author's Chair. Encourage them to think as they listen to one another's essays today about whether they agree or disagree with the author's opinion and whether the essay is convincing enough to change their mind.

4 ▶ **Conduct Author's Chair Sharing**

Have a student read her persuasive essay aloud from the Author's Chair. At the end of the sharing, facilitate a discussion using questions like those that follow, and give the author an opportunity to respond to the class's comments and questions:

Q *What did you learn about [being a vegetarian] from hearing [Christiane's] essay?*

Q *Do you agree or disagree with her opinion? Why?*

Q *Were you persuaded to change your mind from hearing [Christiane's] essay?*

Q *What questions can we ask [Christiane] about what she wrote?*

Follow this procedure to have other students share from the Author's Chair.

5 ▶ **Reflect on Audience Behavior During Author's Chair Sharing**

Ask and briefly discuss:

Q *What did we do well as an audience today? What do we want to work on the next time authors share their work?*

Q *If you shared an essay, did you feel that people were being respectful of your opinions and considering them carefully? Why or why not?*

Assure the students that they will all get to share their published essays from the Author's Chair in the coming days. Explain that after the essays are read aloud you will compile them into a class book and place them in the class library so the students can read them during independent reading time.

FACILITATION TIP

Reflect on your experience over the past three weeks with **avoiding repeating or paraphrasing** students' responses. Does this practice feel natural to you? Are you integrating it into class discussions throughout the school day? What effect is it having on the students? Are they participating more responsibly in class discussions? We encourage you to continue to try this practice and reflect on students' responses as you facilitate class discussions in the future. (See the front matter for special considerations for English Language Learners.)

Teacher Note

If necessary, repeat today's lesson for a few more days, or even another week, to give all of the students time to finish publishing their essays (see Open Weeks in the front matter on page xvi). Students who finish may begin a new piece of writing (persuasive or otherwise) or continue working on a piece of writing they started earlier.

Even if you decide to begin another genre unit immediately, continue to have the students share their persuasive essays from the Author's Chair until everyone has had a chance to do so.

EXTENSION

Publish Persuasive Essays Beyond the Classroom

If students are interested, help them identify and locate people and institutions to whom they might send their persuasive essays. Consider school or community newspapers, people in official capacities, or websites or Web logs online. You can search for websites that publish student writing using the keywords "publishing student writing." The Internet is also a good source for names and addresses. If the essays are to be mailed, you might teach the students to write a brief cover letter to accompany the essays.

Poetry

Poetry

Genre

Poetry

During this three-week unit, the students hear, discuss, and write poetry. They think about what makes a poem a poem and informally explore imagery, sound, and form in poetry. They learn to listen to the language in poems and think about what poems look like on the page. They generate ideas for poems, including writing about objects, weather, things that move or make noise, and months of the year. They learn that poets can break punctuation rules intentionally, and they think about what this would look like in their own poems. They tap into their creativity and express interest in and appreciation for one another's creativity and writing.

Development Across the Grades

Grade	Elements of Poetry	Craft Focus	Skills and Conventions
4	• Creating images using sensory details • Using sound and typography (or shape) in poems to support their meaning	• Simile • Personification • Onomatopoeia, repetition, and alliteration • Rhythm and rhyme	• Exploring how poets follow or intentionally break punctuation rules for poetic effect
5	• Creating images using sensory details • Using sounds and poetic forms to support meaning	• Metaphor, simile • Personification • Rhythm, rhyme, and repetition • Line length	• Exploring how poets follow or intentionally break punctuation rules for poetic effect
6	• Creating images using sensory details • Using sounds and poetic forms to support meaning	• Metaphor, simile • Personification • Rhythm, rhyme, and repetition • Line length	• Exploring how poets follow or intentionally break punctuation rules for poetic effect

UNIT OVERVIEW

WEEK	DAY 1	DAY 2	DAY 3	DAY 4
	Immersion and Drafting			
1	**Exploring Poetry:** "September" **Quick-Write:** Ideas for poems about months	**Exploring Poetry:** "umbrella," "safety pin" **Quick-Write:** Ideas for poems about objects	**Exploring Poetry:** "Child Frightened by a Thunderstorm" **Quick-Write:** Ideas for poems about weather	**Exploring Poetry and Pair Conferring:** "fireworks" **Focus:** Notice poetic forms
2	**Exploring Poetry:** "flamingo" and "crickets" **Focus:** shapes of poems	**Exploring Poetry:** "Windshield Wiper" **Quick-Write:** Ideas for poems about things that move or make noise	**Exploring Poetry:** Excerpt from "The Bells" **Focus:** Repetition for poetic effect	**Exploring Poetry and Pair Conferring:** "I Love the Look of Words" **Quick-Write:** "Words Are Like _____."
	Revision, Proofreading, and Publication			
3	**Selecting and Revising Drafts** **Focus:** Image, sound, and form	**Proofreading** **Focus:** Intentionally breaking the rules	**Publishing** **Focus:** Author's Chair sharing	**Publishing** **Focus:** Expressing interest in and appreciation for one another's writing

GENRE: POETRY

"September"
by John Updike
(see page 573)

Fall sensations pervade this poem about September.

"umbrella," "safety pin," and "fireworks"
by Valerie Worth
(see pages 574, 575, 577)

Personification, sound, and imagery are represented in three small poems.

"Child Frightened by a Thunderstorm"
by Ted Kooser
(see page 576)

Thunder takes on a menacing personality in this poem.

Writing Focus

- Students hear, discuss, and write poems.

- Students think about what a poem is.

- Students explore imagery, sound, and form in poems.

- Students generate and quick-write ideas for poems.

- Students cultivate their creativity.

Social Focus

- Students listen respectfully to the thinking of others and share their own.

- Students express interest in and appreciation for one another's writing.

DO AHEAD

- Prior to Day 1, decide how you will randomly assign partners to work together during the unit. See the front matter for suggestions about assigning partners randomly (see page xiii) and for considerations for pairing English Language Learners (see page xxviii).

See the front matter for suggestions about assigning partners randomly (see page xiii) and for considerations for pairing English Language Learners (see page xxviii).

TEACHER AS WRITER

"Poetry is the language of extremity.… You feel something potent and then you transfer it onto the page."
— *Li-Young Lee*

This week take time to find and read some poems. You might look for poems in books in the library, in magazines, online, and on your own bookshelves at home. As you read, ask yourself, "What makes a poem a poem?" Write your thoughts in your writing notebook and add to it as you get new ideas.

Day 1

Materials

- "September" (see page 573)
- *Student Writing Handbook* page 36
- Two sheets of chart paper and a marker

Exploring Poetry

In this lesson, the students:

- Work with a new partner
- Hear and discuss a poem
- Think about what makes a poem a poem
- Explore sensory details and images in poems
- Quick-write ideas for poems about months of the year

Immersion in Poetry

In this unit, the students generate ideas and write poems using published poems as models and sources of inspiration. They learn that poems use words and images to communicate feelings and create vivid mental pictures in the reader's mind. They develop an intuitive understanding of what poetry is by exploring *images* (for example, sensory details, metaphor, personification), *sounds* (for example, repetition, alliteration, onomatopoeia), and *forms* (for example, open and closed). While the learning of literary terms is not emphasized at grade 5, exploring these concepts and how they function in poems is.

The students are encouraged to activate their imaginations and take creative risks in this unit. They see how poets often create their own rules and even intentionally break rules for poetic effect. They learn that poetry gives writers endless freedom in using words to express their ideas.

Teacher Note

The partners you assign today will stay together for the unit.

Making Meaning® Teacher

You can either have the students work with their current *Making Meaning* partner or assign them new partners for this unit.

GETTING READY TO WRITE

 Pair Students and Discuss Working Together

Randomly assign partners (see "Do Ahead" on page 549) and make sure they know each other's names. Gather the class with partners sitting together, facing you. Have the students bring their writing notebooks, *Student Writing Handbooks*, and pencils with them.

Explain that over the next three weeks partners will work together to explore writing poetry. Ask:

 Q *What have you learned about being a good partner? Turn and tell your partner what you will do to be a good partner to him or her.*

After a moment for partners to talk, signal for their attention and discuss as a class:

Q *What did your partner say he or she will do to be a good partner to you?*

Encourage partners to keep these things in mind as they start working together today.

2 ▶ Introduce Poetry

Ask the students to flip through their *Student Writing Handbooks* and to stop on any page that has a poem on it. After a moment, signal for their attention. Ask partners to look at each other's pages to see if they agree that they have both stopped on poems. Ask and briefly discuss as a class:

Q *How do you know that what you stopped on is a poem?*

Q *What do you think makes a poem a poem?*

> **Students might say:**
>
> "I know it's a poem because it has lots of short lines."
>
> "I know it's a poem because it has rhyming words."
>
> "A poem doesn't take up the whole page, like a story."
>
> "In addition to what [Pilar] said, I think a poem gives you a picture in your head."

Explain that you will read a poem aloud today, and encourage the students to continue to think about what makes a poem a poem as they listen.

◀ **Teacher Note**

To review the procedure for "Turn to Your Partner," see volume 1, page xiv.

◀ **Teacher Note**

Regularly remind the students to use the discussion prompts they learned when they participate in class discussions. The prompts are:

- "I agree with _____ because…"
- "I disagree with _____ because…"
- "In addition to what _____ said, I think…"

3▶ Read and Discuss "September"

Ask the students to close their handbooks and listen as you read "September" aloud. Invite them to imagine what is happening in this poem as they listen.

Read the poem (including the title) aloud twice, slowly and clearly. Clarify vocabulary on the first reading.

Teacher Note

To review the procedure for defining vocabulary during the reading, see volume 1, page 8. ▶

Suggested Vocabulary

brush: dead leaves, twigs, and branches

ELL Vocabulary

English Language Learners may benefit from discussing additional vocabulary, including:

well-honeyed: with lots of honey

chrysanthemums: a kind of flower that blooms in the fall

suds: soap bubbles

Ask:

Q *What did you imagine as you listened to this poem? Turn to your partner.*

Have a few volunteers share their thinking with the class. Ask the students to turn to *Student Writing Handbook* page 36, where "September" is reproduced, and to reread the poem for themselves. After a moment, ask:

Teacher Note ▶

If necessary, explain that an *image* in a poem is something that creates a mental picture.

Q *What words or images does the poet include to help you see what the month of September is like? Hear? Feel? Smell or taste?*

Students might say:

"The words 'breezes taste of apple peel' make me imagine tasting apples and feeling the breeze on my face."

"I hear the bee buzzing when I read, 'The bee, his hive well-honeyed, hums.'"

"'New books, erasers, and chalk' make me think of the first day of school. That happens in September."

Point out that the poet uses *sensory details*, or words and images that help us imagine using our senses. Explain that most poems contain sensory details; they are one thing that makes a poem a poem. Title a sheet of chart paper "Notes About Poems," and underneath write *Poems have sensory details that help us see, hear, smell, taste, and feel what's happening.*

Ask:

Q　*What else do you think makes "September" a poem?*

As the students report, record their ideas on the chart. If the students suggest ideas that apply to some (but not all) poems, begin these chart entries with the word *sometimes* (for example, *Sometimes poems rhyme*, and *Sometimes poems have short lines*). Explain that you will continue to add to the chart in the coming days.

4　**Quick-Write: Ideas for Poems About Months**

Use "Think, Pair, Share" to have partners first think about and then discuss:

Q　*Imagine that we are writing a poem like "September" for the month of July. What words and images might we include in the poem to help a reader see, hear, smell, taste, and feel the month of July?* [pause] *Turn to your partner.*

After partners have discussed the question, signal for their attention and call on a few volunteers to share their ideas with the class. As they report, record their ideas on a sheet of chart paper entitled "Ideas About July."

◀　**Teacher Note**

To review the procedure for "Think, Pair, Share," see volume 1, page xiv.

 Note

If necessary, simplify this question by rephrasing it in the following way:

Q　*The poem we read is about September. Let's think about another month. What is the month of July like?*

Q　*What do you do in July? What do you see? Hear? Feel?*

Ideas About July

- melting ice cream cone

- short pants

- splashing, dripping

- wet bathing suit

- the smell of pool water

- toes in the hot sand

Explain that the students will choose another month of the year and quick-write words and images they could include in a poem about that month. Have them open to the next blank page in the writing ideas section of their notebooks and write their ideas for 5 minutes. Encourage them to quickly write whatever ideas come to mind.

When time is up, signal for the students' attention and have a few volunteers share their list of words and images with the class. Explain that during writing time today the students may continue to add to this list, write words and images for a different month, or write about anything they choose.

WRITING TIME

5 ▶ **Write Independently**

Ask the students to return to their seats. Write the following choices on the board and have them write silently for 20–30 minutes.

- Add to the list you started in the quick-write.

- Write words and images for a different month.

- Write about anything you choose.

If necessary, remind them that during silent writing time there should be no talking, whispering, or walking around. Join the

Teacher Note ▶

Note that on Days 1–3 of this week, the students may write poems or anything else they choose. On Day 4, after exposure to several more poems, all the students will be asked to begin writing in this genre.

students in writing for a few minutes; then walk around the room and observe.

Signal to let the students know when writing time is over.

SHARING AND REFLECTING

6 ▶ **Share Writing and Reflect**

Ask partners to talk briefly about what they wrote today. After a moment, signal for their attention and ask:

Q   *What did your partner write about today?*

Q   *What did you and your new partner do to work well together when talking and sharing your writing?*

◀ **Teacher Note**

Save the "Notes About Poems" chart to use on Day 2 and throughout the unit. Display the "Ideas About July" chart throughout the unit.

Day 2

Materials

- "umbrella" (see page 574)
- "safety pin" (see page 575)
- "Notes About Poems" chart from Day 1
- *Student Writing Handbook* pages 37–38

Exploring Poetry

In this lesson, the students:

- Hear and discuss poems
- Explore sensory details and images in poems
- Quick-write ideas for poems about objects
- Informally explore metaphor and personification
- Speak clearly and listen to one another
- Discuss and solve problems that arise in their work together

Literary Concepts in Grade 5

In this unit the students informally explore the following literary concepts. This work prepares them for more formal instruction about literary terms in poetry in subsequent grades. Keep in mind that defining and using the terms themselves is not emphasized in this unit.

- *alliteration:* repeating consonant sounds in successive words ("Sing a song of sixpence…")

- *metaphor:* a direct or indirect assertion that a thing is something else ("Life is a broken-winged bird that cannot fly.")

- *meter:* a fixed, regular rhythm in a poem ("Two roads diverged in a yellow wood…")

- *onomatopoeia:* representing something using words that imitate the sounds associated with it (*splash, pitter-patter, tick-tock*)

- *personification:* endowing a thing or an animal with human characteristics ("The wind stood up and gave a shout.")

- *repetition:* repeating words or phrases for poetic effect ("Bells, bells, bells")

- *rhyme:* words ending with the same sound (*twinkle* and *sprinkle*)

- *rhythm:* pattern of stresses and pauses in a poem

- *simile:* a comparison of two things, connected by words such as *like* and *as* ("My love is like a red, red rose.")

GETTING READY TO WRITE

1 ▸ Briefly Review Poetry

Gather the class with partners sitting together, facing you. Have the students bring their notebooks, *Student Writing Handbooks*, and pencils with them.

Review that yesterday the students began exploring poetry. They read the poem "September" and brainstormed words and images for other months of the year. Briefly review the items on the "Notes About Poems" chart. Remind the students that you will add items to the chart throughout the unit.

2 ▸ Read and Discuss "umbrella"

Ask the students to close their eyes and create a picture in their minds as they listen to a poem. Read "umbrella" (including the title) aloud twice, slowly and clearly.

ELL Vocabulary

English Language Learners may benefit from discussing the following vocabulary:

slack: loose

moping: acting in a sad way

hatching a plot: making a plan

furious: very angry

Ask the students to open their *Student Writing Handbooks* to page 37, where "umbrella" is reproduced, and to reread the poem for themselves. After a moment, ask:

Q *What sensory details do you notice in "umbrella" that help you imagine what's happening?*

Students might say:

"I hear flapping when I read 'flap out and escape.'"

"I agree with [Penelope]. The words 'furious sweep of the storm' make me imagine the umbrella flying out in the wind and the rain."

Point out that the poet writes about the umbrella as if it is alive, and that writing about objects as if they are alive is a common thing that poets do. Ask:

Q *What words does Valerie Worth use to write about the umbrella as if it's alive?*

Students might say:

"She says the umbrella is 'sleeping' or 'moping.'"

"The word *claw* makes me imagine the umbrella hanging on like a bird or a bat."

"'In addition to what [Tremaine] said, it's 'hatching a plot' to escape."

3 ▶ Read and Discuss "safety pin"

Ask the students to turn to *Student Writing Handbook* page 38 and to follow along as you read another poem in which the poet writes about an object as if it is alive. Read "safety pin" aloud twice (including the title), slowly and clearly. Ask and briefly discuss:

Q *What words does the poet use to write as if the safety pin is alive?*

Q *What sensory details do you notice in these poems that help you imagine what's happening?*

Students might say:

"The poet uses 'sleeps on its side quietly,' as if it's sleeping like a baby."

"She says that the safety pin is like 'a small fish' and 'a thin shrimp.'"

"'In addition to what [Jorge] said, it 'looks at the sharp point with a surprised eye.' A real safety pin can't look at things or be surprised."

"'When the safety pin 'snaps its tail out like a thin shrimp,' I imagine a snap! and the safety pin swimming away like a shrimp."

4 ▶ Quick-Write: Ideas for Poems About Objects

Ask and have the students think quietly to themselves about:

Q *If you were going to write a poem about an object in the classroom, what might it be?*

Ask the students to get an object they are thinking about and carry it back to their seat with their writing materials. If they are not able to carry the object back to their seat, have them sit where they can see it. When all of the students have selected their object, ask the following questions one at a time and have the students think quietly to themselves about them.

Q   *What words might you use to describe what your object looks like? Sounds like? Smells like? Feels like?*

Q   *If your object came to life, what might it do?*

After students have had a chance to think, signal for their attention. Have them open to the next blank page in their notebooks, write the name of the object at the top of the page, and quick-write some ideas for what they could include in a poem about that object.

Have the students write for 3–4 minutes; then signal for their attention and have a couple of volunteers share their ideas with the class. After sharing, ask the students to resume writing for a few more minutes.

Signal for the students' attention and call on a few volunteers to share what they wrote.

> **Students might say:**
>
> "My object is a stapler. I wrote that it is long, gray, and cold, and that it chews through a sheet of paper."
>
> "I wrote that my pencil is wearing a yellow jumpsuit and dances around on the paper."

Direct the students' attention to the "Notes About Poems" chart and add *Poems can be about anything* and *You can write about objects as if they are alive.*

Explain that during writing time today the students may continue what they started during the quick-write, continue brainstorming words and images for months of the year (from Day 1), or write about anything they choose.

WRITING TIME

▶5 Write Independently

Write the following choices on the board:

- Continue writing what you started during the quick-write.

- Continue to write words and images for months of the year.

- Write about anything you choose.

Have the students return to their seats and write silently for
20–30 minutes. Join the students in writing for a few minutes;
then walk around the room and observe.

Signal to let the students know when writing time is over.

SHARING AND REFLECTING

▶6 Share Writing and Reflect

Ask partners to talk together briefly about what they wrote today.
After a moment, signal for their attention and ask:

Q　*What did your partner write about today?*

Q　*Did you or your partner write about an object? Read us what
you wrote.*

Q　*What problems did you and your partner have working together
today? What will you do to avoid those problems next time?*

Day 3

Exploring Poetry

In this lesson, the students:

- Hear and discuss poems
- Explore sensory details and images in a poem
- Informally explore metaphor and personification
- Explore how word sounds function in a poem
- Quick-write ideas for poems about weather

GETTING READY TO WRITE

1 ▶ ### Discuss Rhyme in Poetry

Gather the class with partners sitting together, facing you. Have the students bring their notebooks, *Student Writing Handbooks*, and pencils with them.

Review that this week the students have been exploring poetry. They have read and heard three poems ("September," "umbrella," and "safety pin"). Have the students open to *Student Writing Handbook* pages 36–38 and briefly review the poems. Ask:

Q *What do you notice about the rhyming patterns in these three poems?*

If necessary, point out that "umbrella" and "safety pin" have no predictable rhyming pattern, while "September" has two lines that rhyme in each stanza. On the "Notes About Poems" chart, add *Some poems have rhyming patterns and some don't.*

Briefly review other items on the chart and ask the students to listen for rhymes and the other things listed as they hear a new poem today.

Materials

- "Child Frightened by a Thunderstorm" (see page 576)
- "Notes About Poems" chart
- *Student Writing Handbook* pages 36–39
- *Assessment Resource Book*

 Note

You might provide the prompt "I notice…" to your English Language Learners to help them verbalize their responses to this question.

2 ▶ Read and Discuss "Child Frightened by a Thunderstorm"

Ask the students to close their eyes as they listen to you read "Child Frightened by a Thunderstorm" aloud. Invite them to imagine what is happening as they listen.

Read the poem (including the title) aloud once, slowly and clearly. Clarify vocabulary as you read.

> **Suggested Vocabulary**
>
> **peonies:** a kind of flower
> **shears:** scissors
>
>
>
> **ELL Vocabulary**
>
> English Language Learners may benefit from discussing additional vocabulary, including:
>
> **nested:** made a nest
> **bouquets:** bunches of flowers

Ask the students to open their *Student Writing Handbooks* to page 39, where "Child Frightened by a Thunderstorm" is reproduced, and to reread the poem for themselves. After a moment, ask:

Q　*What do you notice about how this poet writes about thunder?*

> **Students might say:**
>
> "He writes as if the thunder is alive."
>
> "I agree with [Lowell]. He says the thunder 'snipped bouquets of branches for its bed.' That's what a person or an animal would do."
>
> "In addition to what [Amy] said, he describes the thunder like a giant bird. It has wings and a beak and red eyes."

As the students share, refer to any items they mention on the "Notes About Poems" chart, if appropriate.

Teacher Note ▶

If the students have difficulty answering this question, suggest some ideas like those in the "Students might say" note, and then ask "What else do you notice?"

3 ▶ **Discuss Word Sounds in the Poem**

Point out that poets often include words that sound like what the poem is about. Ask:

Q *What does thunder sound like?*

Students might say:

"Thunder goes BOOM!"

"Rumble, rumble, rumble"

"Crash!"

Ask the students to read the poem aloud with you, paying attention to the sound of the words as they read. Invite them to listen for words that remind them of the sound of thunder.

Read the poem aloud; then ask:

 Q *What words in the poem remind you of the sound of thunder? Turn to your partner.*

Have a few volunteers share their thinking with the class. On the "Notes About Poems" chart, add *Poems can include words that sound like what the poem is about.*

◀ **Teacher Note**

Words in the poem with sounds reminiscent of thunder include *rumpled*, *crushed*, and *clattering*.

▶ **Quick-Write: Ideas for Poems About Weather**

Ask and briefly discuss:

Q *If you were going to write a poem like "Child Frightened by a Thunderstorm," only about another kind of weather, what kind of weather might you write about?*

Students might say:

"Wind"

"Snow"

"Tornadoes"

"A hot, sunny day"

"Foggy days"

Ask the students to open to the next blank page of their notebooks and write the name of the type of weather they are thinking about at the top of the page. Have them think quietly to themselves about the following questions as you ask them one at a time:

Q *What words or images might you use to describe what that weather looks like? Sounds like? Feels like? Smells or tastes like?*

Q *What might you do in that kind of weather?*

After the students have had a chance to think, have partners share their thinking. After a moment, signal for their attention and have them quick-write some ideas for what they could include in a poem about that kind of weather.

Have the students write for 3–4 minutes; then signal for their attention and have a couple of volunteers share their ideas with the class. After sharing, ask the students to resume writing for a few more minutes.

Signal for the students' attention and ask a few volunteers to share what they wrote.

> **Students might say:**
>
> "I thought about rain. I wrote the words *mud puddle, dripping umbrella, splash,* and *pitter-patter.*"
>
> "I wrote about snow. I thought of words that mean 'cold,' like *freezing, icy,* and *shivering.*"

Explain that during writing time today the students may continue what they started during the quick-write, continue writing ideas for poems about objects or months of the year, or write about anything they choose.

WRITING TIME

 5 ▶ Write Independently

Write the following choices on the board:

- Continue writing what you started during the quick-write.

- Continue to write ideas for poems about objects or months of the year.

- Write about anything you choose.

Ask the students to return to their seats and have them write silently for 20–30 minutes. Join the students in writing for a few minutes; then walk around the room and observe.

> ### CLASS ASSESSMENT NOTE
>
> Observe the students and ask yourself:
>
> - Do the students seem to be writing freely and creatively?
>
> - Are they engaged in their writing?
>
> - Do they seem overly cautious or inhibited about what they put on paper?
>
> After about 10 minutes, support students who are struggling to start by asking them questions such as:
>
> **Q** *What kind of weather could you write about?*
>
> **Q** *What sensory details can you write to describe what [a windy day] sounds like? Looks like? Feels like?*
>
> **Q** *What does [wind] sound like? What words make you think of the sound of [wind]?*
>
> Record your observations in the *Assessment Resource Book*.

Signal to let the students know when writing time is over.

SHARING AND REFLECTING

 ## Share Writing and Reflect

Ask partners to talk together briefly about what they wrote today. After a moment, signal for their attention and ask:

Q *What did your partner write about today?*

Q *Did you or your partner write ideas about weather? Read us what you wrote.*

Explain that all of the students will start writing poems tomorrow, and they will continue to draft poems for the coming week. Tell them that they will eventually select one of their poems to improve, revise, and publish in a class collection of poetry.

Day 4

Exploring Poetry and Pair Conferring

In this lesson, the students:

- Hear, discuss, and write poems
- Think about what poems look like on the page
- Explore how word sounds function in a poem
- Express interest in and appreciation for one another's writing

GETTING READY TO WRITE

1▶ Explore Form in Poetry

Have partners sit together at desks today. Review that this week the students read the poems "September," "umbrella," "safety pin," and "Child Frightened by a Thunderstorm" and thought about what makes a poem a poem. Point out that one thing that makes a poem a poem is what it looks like on the page.

Explain that you would like one partner in each pair to open his *Student Writing Handbook* to pages 36–37, while the other partner opens her *Student Writing Handbook* to pages 38–39. By laying the books side by side, each pair should be able to see all four poems from this week.

Materials

- "fireworks" (see page 577)
- "Child Frightened by a Thunderstorm" from Day 3
- "umbrella" and "safety pin" from Day 2
- "September" from Day 1
- "Notes About Poems" chart
- *Student Writing Handbook* pages 36–40
- "Conference Notes" record sheet for each student (BLM1)

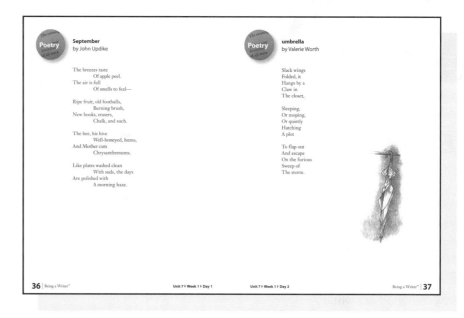

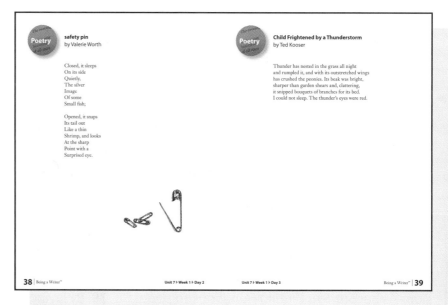

Ask:

Q *What do you notice about how these poems look on the page?*

Q *How do they look similar? How do they look different?*

Point out that some poems have short lines (as in "September," "umbrella," and "safety pin") and others have long lines (as in "Child Frightened by a Thunderstorm"). Also point out that some poems have *stanzas*, or sections separated by a space, while others do not. Ask:

Q *What do you notice about the stanzas in each of these poems?*

Students might say:

"I notice that in 'September' there are four stanzas with four lines each."

"In 'umbrella' all three stanzas have five lines each. Some lines are just one word."

"I agree with [Wen]. The poem 'safety pin' has two stanzas and each one has seven lines."

"'Child Frightened by a Thunderstorm' doesn't have any stanzas."

Direct the students' attention to the "Notes About Poems" chart. Add *Poems can have short or long lines, Some poems have stanzas,* and *Poems can have the same number of lines in each stanza.*

2 Read and Discuss "fireworks"

Ask the students to close their eyes as they listen to you read "fireworks" aloud. Invite them to listen for sounds and images that help them imagine fireworks.

Read the poem (including the title) aloud once, slowly and clearly.

ELL Vocabulary

English Language Learners may benefit from discussing the following vocabulary:

climbs: goes up

flare: burst of fire

invisible: not seen

Ask the students to open their *Student Writing Handbooks* to page 40, where "fireworks" is reproduced, and to reread the poem for themselves. Ask and briefly discuss:

Q *What do you notice about how this poem looks on the page? Why do you think it looks that way?*

Students might say:

"Some lines are short and some are long."

"I agree with [Tori]. The lines start out short and get longer and longer."

"It has the shape of a slide."

"In addition to what [Victor] said, this poem doesn't have any stanzas."

Q *What sensory details help you see and hear these fireworks? Turn to your partner.*

 Q *What words in this poem remind you of the sound of fireworks? Turn to your partner.*

Teacher Note ▶

Remind the students to double-space all writing in their notebooks so they have space to revise later, if necessary.

Explain that today you would like the students all to pick one of the five poems they read this week and try writing a poem that looks similar to it on the page. Encourage them to write poems using their quick-write ideas from earlier in the week. They may also write poems about any other topics they choose. Review the items on the "Notes About Poems" chart, and encourage the students to use some of these ideas in their poems.

WRITING TIME

Teacher Note

You may want to shorten today's writing time to leave more time for the pair conferences in Step 4. ▶

3 **Draft Poems in Their Notebooks**

Have the students write poems silently for 20–30 minutes. If necessary, remind them to write their drafts, double-spaced, in their notebooks. Join the students in writing for a few minutes; then begin conferring with individual students.

TEACHER CONFERENCE NOTE

Over the coming two weeks, confer individually with your students about the poems they are writing. Ask each student to show you a draft of a poem and to read it aloud to you. Ask yourself:

- Is this student attempting to write a poem, rather than a story?

- Does he include sensory details?

- What other elements of poetry does he try to include in his poem?

continues

TEACHER CONFERENCE NOTE *continued*

Support students by asking them questions such as:

Q *What is this poem about?*

Q *What sensory details [are you including/can you include]? How will that help your reader imagine what's happening?*

Q *Tell me about the lines and stanzas in your poem.*

Q *What sounds are you thinking about as you write your poem?*

Document your observations for each student on the "Conference Notes" record sheet (BLM1). Use the "Conference Notes" record sheets during conferences throughout this unit.

Signal to let the students know when writing time is over.

SHARING AND REFLECTING

Confer in Pairs About Poems

Gather the class with partners sitting together, facing you. Explain that partners will read what they wrote today to each other and confer about it. Ask:

Q *What would you like your partner to do to show that he or she is interested in your writing and your creative ideas?*

Students might say:

"I would like my partner to listen as I read my poem."

"I would like my partner to ask me questions about the poem."

"I would like my partner to tell me the part he likes."

"I would like my partner to notice the sensory details I used."

Have partners share their writing with each other.

Observe the students closely and provide sufficient time for both partners to share their writing before signaling for their attention.

◀ **Teacher Note**

If necessary, signal the students about halfway through sharing time so partners can switch roles if they have not yet done so.

Reflect on Pair Conferences and Poems

Help the students reflect on their work today by asking:

Q *What did your partner do to show interest in your writing and creative ideas?*

Q *What did you do to show interest in your partner's writing?*

Q *What sensory details did your partner include in her poem? What did you imagine from those details?*

Explain that the students will continue to draft poems during the coming week.

EXTENSION

Continue to Explore Poems

Gather collections of poetry and make these available for the students to read during independent reading time. Also read poems aloud and invite the students to select and read aloud poems they like. Take time to discuss the poems by asking:

Q *What sensory details did you notice in the poem? What did that detail make you imagine?*

Poetry

September

by John Updike

The breezes taste
      Of apple peel.
The air is full
      Of smells to feel—

Ripe fruit, old footballs,
      Burning brush,
New books, erasers,
      Chalk, and such.

The bee, his hive
      Well-honeyed, hums,
And Mother cuts
      Chrysanthemums.

Like plates washed clean
      With suds, the days
Are polished with
      A morning haze.

Poetry

umbrella
by Valerie Worth

Slack wings
Folded, it
Hangs by a
Claw in
The closet,

Sleeping,
Or moping,
Or quietly
Hatching
A plot

To flap out
And escape
On the furious
Sweep of
The storm.

Poetry

safety pin
by Valerie Worth

Closed, it sleeps
On its side
Quietly,
The silver
Image
Of some
Small fish;

Opened, it snaps
Its tail out
Like a thin
Shrimp, and looks
At the sharp
Point with a
Surprised eye.

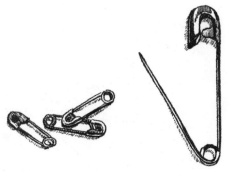

Child Frightened by a Thunderstorm
by Ted Koozer

Thunder has nested in the grass all night
and rumpled it, and with its outstretched wings
has crushed the peonies. Its beak was bright,
sharper than garden shears and, clattering,
it snipped its bouquets of branches for its bed.
I could not sleep. The thunder's eyes were red.

Poetry

fireworks

by Valerie Worth

First
A far thud,
Then the rocket
Climbs the air,
A dull red flare,
To hang, a moment,
Invisible, before
Its shut black shell cracks
And claps against the ears,
Breaks and billows into bloom,
Spilling down clear green sparks, gold spears,
Silent sliding silver waterfalls and stars.

GENRE: POETRY

"flamingo" and "crickets"
by Valerie Worth
(see pages 600 and 601)

The shapes of these two poems help to communicate their meaning.

"Windshield Wiper"
by Eve Merriam
(see page 602)

Sound, shape, and repetition weave together to tell about windshield wipers.

Excerpt from "The Bells"
by Edgar Allan Poe
(see page 603)

Repetition brings the bells alive in this excerpt from Poe's classic poem.

"I Love the Look of Words"
by Maya Angelou
(see page 604)

Words tumble like popcorn onto the page.

Writing Focus

- Students hear, discuss, and write poems.

- Students explore imagery, sound, and form in poems.

- Students generate and quick-write ideas for poems.

- Students cultivate their creativity.

- Students confer with one another and the teacher.

Social Focus

- Students listen respectfully to the thinking of others and share their own.

- Students help one another improve their writing.

- Students express interest in and appreciation for one another's writing.

Rain
Like a drummer's brush,
the rain hushes the surface
of tin porches.
            — Emanuel de Pasquale

Read the poem above aloud and listen to the sounds of the words. Ask yourself: How do the sounds of the words support the meaning of the poem?

This week try writing some short poems that include words with sounds that support the meaning of your poem. If helpful, use the poem above as a model. Here's another example:

Wind
Like a magician's whip,
the wind whistles and flaps
the white sheets.

Day 1

Materials

- "flamingo" and "crickets" (see pages 600–601)
- "Notes About Poems" chart
- *Student Writing Handbook* page 36–42

Exploring Poetry

In this lesson, the students:

- Hear, discuss, and write poems
- Think about what poems look like on the page
- Explore how word sounds function in a poem
- Explore sensory details and images in a poem
- Informally explore metaphor and personification
- Get ideas by listening to others

GETTING READY TO WRITE

 Briefly Review Poetry

Gather the class with partners sitting together, facing you. Have them bring their *Student Writing Handbooks* with them.

Review that last week the students began exploring poetry. Ask the students to review pages 36–40 of their *Student Writing Handbooks* and to scan the five poems they read last week. Ask and briefly discuss:

Q *What do you remember learning about poetry last week?*

Briefly review the items on the "Notes About Poems" chart. Explain that the students will hear and read more poems this week. Invite them to look for items listed on the chart as they read.

 Read and Discuss "flamingo" and "crickets"

Ask the students to close their *Student Writing Handbooks* and to listen to the sounds of the words as you read two poems aloud. Read "flamingo" aloud twice, slowly and clearly.

ELL Vocabulary

English Language Learners may benefit from discussing the following vocabulary:

lingers: moves slowly
ponders: thinks

Ask:

Q *What sounds did you hear over and over in this poem? Turn to your partner.*

Without discussing as a class, ask the students to close their eyes again and listen. Read "crickets" aloud twice, slowly and clearly. Ask:

Q *What letters or sounds did you hear over and over in this poem? Turn to your partner.*

Ask the students to open their *Student Writing Handbooks* to pages 41–42, where "flamingo" and "crickets" are reproduced, and to reread the poems aloud to themselves. After a moment, ask:

Q *What do you notice about the sounds of the words in these poems?*

Q *How do the sounds of the words in ["crickets"] help you imagine a [cricket]?*

Students might say:

"I hear *t* and *k* in 'crickets.' Those sounds remind me of the sound that crickets make."

"I notice that there are a lot of *l* sounds in the poem 'flamingo.' The word *flamingo* has an *l* in it."

"In addition to what [Marcus] said, maybe the poet used *l* sounds because the letter *l* is a tall, thin letter, like a flamingo."

Discuss the Shapes of Poems

Ask and briefly discuss:

Q *What do you notice about the shapes of these two poems?*

FACILITATION TIP

Continue to focus on **responding neutrally with interest** during class discussions by refraining from overtly praising or criticizing the students' responses. Instead, build the students' intrinsic motivation by responding with genuine curiosity and interest; for example:

● *"Interesting—say more about that."*

● *"What you said makes me curious. I wonder…"*

● *"You have a point of view that's [similar to/different from] what [Jackson] just said. How is it [similar/different]?"*

Q *How does the shape of the poem "flamingo" help you imagine a flamingo?*

Q *Why do you think the poet might have shaped "crickets" this way?*

Students might say:

"Both poems are tall and skinny. The poem 'flamingo' only has one word in each line."

"I agree with [Fiona]. The poem 'crickets' has a couple of lines with more than one word, but most of the lines are one-word lines."

"The shape of the poem 'flamingo' makes me think of a flamingo standing on one tall leg."

"Maybe the poet shaped 'crickets' like this because when you read one line at a time, it could sound like a cricket chirping."

Point out that poets are intentional about what their poems look like on the page and that the shape of a poem can help the reader understand what the poem is about. On the "Notes About Poems" chart, add *A poem's shape can help us understand what it's about.*

Explain that the students will continue to write poems today, and that they may try writing poems that look like "flamingo" and "cricket," if they wish. Remind the students to refer to the "Notes About Poems" chart to get ideas for their poems.

WRITING TIME

 4 Write Independently

Have the students return to their seats to write poems silently for 20–30 minutes. Join the students in writing for a few minutes; then confer with individual students.

TEACHER CONFERENCE NOTE

As you did on Day 4 of last week, confer individually with your students about the poems they are writing. Ask each student to show you a draft of a poem and to read it aloud to you. Ask yourself:

- Is this student attempting to write a poem rather than a story?

- Does he include sensory details?

- What other elements of poetry does he try to include in his poem?

Support students by asking them questions such as:

Q *What is this poem about?*

Q *What sensory details [are you including/can you include]? How will that help your reader imagine what's happening?*

Q *Tell me about the lines and stanzas in your poem.*

Q *What sounds are you thinking about as you write your poem?*

Document your observations for each student on the "Conference Notes" record sheet (BLM1).

Signal to let the students know when writing time is over.

SHARING AND REFLECTING

▶ Reflect on Creativity

Remind the students that poets must tap into their creativity to write poems that readers can really imagine and enjoy. Creativity, the ability to create something new or to recreate something familiar in a new way, helps them write unique poems about ordinary things like birds and crickets.

Ask the students to review the poetry they wrote today and to choose one line to share with the class. Encourage them to choose a line they like or that they believe shows their creativity. After a moment, go around the room and have each student read her line aloud, without comment.

After the students have read their lines, facilitate discussion among the students by asking:

Q *What lines did you hear that got your imagination going?*

Q *What made you feel as if you could really sense what was being described?*

Q *What questions do you want to ask a classmate about his or her writing?*

Explain that the students will continue to work on poems tomorrow.

Day 2

Exploring Poetry

Materials

- "Windshield Wiper" (see page 602)
- "Notes About Poems" chart
- *Student Writing Handbook* page 43
- Chart paper and a marker

In this lesson, the students:

- Hear, discuss, and write poems
- Think about what poems look like on the page
- Explore how repetition functions in a poem
- Explore sensory details and images in a poem
- Informally explore rhythm in a poem
- Quick-write ideas for poems

GETTING READY TO WRITE

1 ▶ Explore Elements of Poetry

Gather the class with partners sitting together, facing you. Have the students bring their notebooks, *Student Writing Handbooks*, and pencils with them.

Review that the students have been thinking about sensory details and sounds in poems, as well as what poems look like on the page. Ask the students to open their notebooks and briefly review the poems they have written. Ask and briefly discuss:

Q *What is an interesting sensory detail you have written? Read that detail aloud to us.*

Q *What sounds have you intentionally included in a poem? Read us a few words with that sound.*

Q *What decisions have you made about what a poem looks like on the page? Show us the poem and tell us about your decision.*

2 ▶ Read and Discuss "Windshield Wiper"

Ask the students to open to *Student Writing Handbook* page 43 and to follow along quietly as you read this poem aloud. Invite them to think about what this poet might be trying to do.

Read "Windshield Wiper" aloud once, slowly and clearly. Clarify vocabulary as you read.

> **Suggested Vocabulary**
>
> **bumbershoot:** funny word for umbrella
>
> **ELL Vocabulary**
>
> English Language Learners may benefit from discussing additional vocabulary, including:
>
> **downpour:** heavy rain
> **macintosh:** raincoat

Read the poem aloud again, this time having the students read aloud with you. Ask and briefly discuss:

Q *What do you notice about this poem? Turn to your partner.*

Q *How does the shape of this poem help you understand what it's about?*

Q *What does this poem sound like? How does the poet create that sound?*

Students might say:

"I notice that the poem has two sides, just like there are two windshield wipers on a car."

"When you read the poem aloud, it sounds like the windshield wipers are going back and forth, back and forth."

"In addition to what [Xavier] said, the poet makes it sound like that because she repeats every line."

Point out that this poet creates the rhythm of windshield wipers by using repetition. On the "Notes About Poems" chart, add *You can use repetition in poems to help the reader imagine something.* Ask:

Q   *What sensory details does the poet include? Why do those details make sense in this poem?*

Students might say:

"Having 'fog smog' and 'tissue paper' makes sense at the beginning because it makes you feel like you can't see out of the window very well."

"At the end of the poem, it stops raining and the window gets clear."

3 ▶ Quick-Write: Ideas for Poems About Things That Move or Make Noise

Ask and have the students think quietly to themselves about:

Q   *"Windshield Wiper" is a poem about something that moves and makes noise. If you were going to write a poem about something that moves or makes noise, what might it be?*

After a moment of quiet thinking, call on just a couple of students to share their thinking with the class. Record their ideas on a sheet of chart paper entitled "Things That Move or Make Noise." Without having the students share too many ideas, have the students open to the next blank page in their notebooks and list more things that move or make noise that they could write a poem about.

After about 5 minutes, signal for the students' attention and have a few volunteers share their thinking with the class. Continue to add their ideas to the "Things That Move or Make Noise" chart.

ELL Note

If necessary, simplify this question by rephrasing it in the following way:

Q   *Windshield wipers move or make noise. What is something else that moves or makes noise?*

> ### Things That Move or Make Noise
>
> - a skateboard
> - a bicycle
> - the bubbles in our fish tank
> - the wheel our hamster runs on
> - a bouncing basketball
> - a seesaw

Explain that during writing time today, the students will continue to write poems. Encourage them to write a poem about something that moves or makes noise, if they wish. Briefly review the "Notes About Poems" chart and encourage them to think about including sensory details, as well as repetition, shapes, and sounds, to help the reader imagine what the poem is about.

WRITING TIME

4 **Write Independently**

Have the students return to their seats and write poems silently for 20–30 minutes. Join them in writing for a few minutes; then confer with individual students.

TEACHER CONFERENCE NOTE

Continue to confer individually with your students about the poems they are writing. Ask each student to show you a draft of a poem and to read it aloud to you. Ask yourself:

- Is this student attempting to write a poem rather than a story?

continues

TEACHER CONFERENCE NOTE *continued*

- Does he include sensory details?

- What other elements of poetry does he try to include in his poem?

Support students by asking them questions such as:

Q *What is this poem about?*

Q *What sensory details [are you including/can you include]? How will that help your reader imagine what's happening?*

Q *Tell me about the lines and stanzas in your poem.*

Q *What sounds are you thinking about as you write your poem?*

Q *Where might you use repetition? How might that help your reader understand your poem? What other sounds are you including?*

Document your observations for each student on the "Conference Notes" record sheet (BLM1).

Signal to let the students know when writing time is over.

SHARING AND REFLECTING

Reflect on Creativity

As you did yesterday, have the students review the poetry they wrote today and choose one line to share with the class. Encourage them to choose a line that they believe shows their creativity. After a moment, go around the room and have each student read his line aloud, without comment.

After the students have read their lines, facilitate discussion among the students by asking:

Q *What lines did you hear that got your imagination going?*

Q *What questions do you want to ask a classmate about his or her writing?*

Explain that the students will continue to work on poems tomorrow.

EXTENSION

Explore Sensing Like a Poet

Collect objects that make sounds; have interesting shapes, colors, or textures; or have unique smells or tastes. Have the students handle, listen to, smell, taste, and/or feel the objects and brainstorm words to describe what they are sensing. Chart the brainstormed words and invite the students to write poems about the objects using the words.

Day 3

Exploring Poetry

Materials

- Excerpt from "The Bells" (see page 603)
- "Notes About Poems" chart
- *Student Writing Handbook* page 44

In this lesson, the students:

- Hear, discuss, and write poems
- Explore sensory details and images in a poem
- Explore how word sounds and repetition function in a poem
- Informally explore rhythm in a poem

GETTING READY TO WRITE

1 Explore Elements of Poetry

Gather the class with partners sitting together, facing you. Have the students bring their notebooks, *Student Writing Handbooks*, and pencils with them.

As you did yesterday, have the students briefly review the poems they have written; then ask and briefly discuss:

Q *What is an interesting sensory detail you have written? Read that detail aloud to us.*

Q *What sounds have you intentionally included in a poem? Read us a few words with that sound.*

Q *What decisions have you made about what a poem looks like on the page? Show us the poem and tell us about your decision.*

Q *Where is a place you used repetition? Read that part to us. Why did you decide to repeat those words?*

Read and Discuss an Excerpt from "The Bells"

Explain that you will read another poem aloud today. Briefly review the "Notes About Poems" chart and ask the students to try to notice how the poet includes some of the items on the chart in this poem.

Ask the students to close their eyes and listen as you read the excerpt from "The Bells" aloud. Read the poem aloud once, slowly and clearly. Clarify vocabulary as you read.

> **Suggested Vocabulary**
>
> **sledges:** large sleds pulled by animals
> **foretells:** predicts
> **crystalline:** like crystal
> **Runic rhyme:** an ancient poem with a secret or mysterious meaning
> **tintinnabulation:** ringing of bells

Have the students turn to *Student Writing Handbook* page 44, where the poem is reproduced. Read the poem aloud again, this time having the students read it aloud with you. Ask and briefly discuss:

 Q *What do you notice about this poem? Turn to your partner.*

Q *What does this poem sound like? How does the poet create that sound?*

Q *Where [else] does the poet use repetition, and why do you think he does this?*

Students might say:

"I notice that this poem has some rhyming words, like *bells*, *foretells*, and *wells*."

"The words make it sound like bells are ringing. You can really hear it when he repeats *bells, bells, bells*."

"The poet also uses repetition with the words *tinkle* and *time*. All those words make it sound like sleigh bells are ringing."

If necessary, point out that the poet uses repetition to help the reader imagine the sound of bells. As the students mention other items that appear on the "Notes About Poems" chart, point these out.

Explain that during writing time today, the students will continue to write poems. Encourage them to try including repetition to create sounds or to help the reader imagine something. Remind the students to refer to the "Notes About Poetry" chart as they write.

WRITING TIME

3 ▶ ## Write Independently

Have the students return to their seats and write poems silently for 20–30 minutes. Join them in writing for a few minutes; then confer with individual students.

TEACHER CONFERENCE NOTE

Continue to confer individually with your students about the poems they are writing. Ask each student to show you a draft of a poem and to read it aloud to you. Ask yourself:

- Is this student attempting to write a poem rather than a story?

- Does she include sensory details?

- What other elements of poetry does she try to include in this poem?

Support students by asking them questions such as:

Q *What is this poem about?*

Q *What sensory details [are you including/can you include]? How will that help your reader imagine what's happening?*

Q *Tell me about the lines and stanzas in your poem.*

Q *What sounds are you thinking about as you write your poem?*

Q *Where might you use repetition? How might that help your reader understand your poem? What other sounds are you including?*

Document your observations for each student on the "Conference Notes" record sheet (BLM1).

Signal to let the students know when writing time is over.

SHARING AND REFLECTING

 Reflect on Creativity

As you did on Days 1 and 2, have the students review the poetry they wrote today and choose one line to share with the class. Encourage them to choose a line that they believe shows their creativity. After a moment, go around the room and have each student read her line aloud, without comment.

After the students have read their lines, facilitate discussion among the students by asking:

Q *What lines did you hear that got your imagination going?*

Q *What questions do you want to ask a classmate about his or her writing?*

Explain that the students will confer in pairs about their poems tomorrow.

Day 4

Exploring Poetry and Pair Conferring

Materials

- "I Love the Look of Words" (see page 604)
- "Notes About Poems" chart
- *Student Writing Handbook* pages 39, 45
- Chart paper and a marker

In this lesson, the students:

- Hear, discuss, and write poems
- Explore sensory details and images in a poem
- Informally explore metaphor
- Quick-write similes for words
- Express interest in and appreciation for one another's writing

GETTING READY TO WRITE

1 Explore Elements of Poetry

Gather the class with partners sitting together, facing you. Have the students bring their notebooks, *Student Writing Handbooks*, and pencils with them.

As you did on Days 2 and 3, have the students briefly review the poems they have written; then ask and briefly discuss:

Q *What is an interesting sensory detail you have written? Read that detail aloud to us.*

Q *What sounds have you intentionally included in a poem? Read us a few words with that sound.*

Q *What decisions have you made about what a poem looks like on the page? Show us the poem and tell us about your decision.*

Q *Where is a place you used repetition? Read that part to us. Why did you decide to repeat those words?*

2 ▶ Read and Discuss "I Love the Look of Words"

Explain that you will read another poem aloud today. Briefly review the "Notes About Poems" chart and ask the students to try to notice how the poet includes some of the items on the chart in this poem.

Ask the students to close their eyes and listen as you read "I Love the Look of Words" aloud. Read the poem aloud once, slowly and clearly.

> **ELL Vocabulary**
>
> English Language Learners may benefit from discussing the following vocabulary:
>
> **skillet:** frying pan
> **gobbles:** eats
> **perfuming:** making something smell like perfume

Have the students turn to *Student Writing Handbook* page 45, where the poem is reproduced. Ask the students to read the poem for themselves. Then ask and briefly discuss:

 Q *What do you notice about this poem? Turn to your partner.*

Q *According to this poet, what is reading like?*

If necessary, point out that reading words is like eating popcorn to this poet. Ask:

Q *What words does this poet use to help us understand that reading words is like eating popcorn?*

> **Students might say:**
>
> "The poet talks about how 'black words leap' from the page like 'popcorn leaps' from the pan."
>
> "Her brain gobbles them up just like her mouth gobbles up popcorn.'"
>
> "It says that the ideas from the words stick to her like the smell of butter after she eats popcorn."

Explain that poets commonly write about one thing as if it is like another thing, or as if it is another thing. In this poem, words are like popcorn. In the poem "Child Frightened by a Thunderstorm" from last week (if necessary, have the students turn to handbook page 39), the thunder is a giant bird with red eyes.

On the "Notes About Poems" chart, add *Poets commonly write about one thing as if it is like another.*

3 Quick-Write: "Words Are Like _____"

Write the words *Words Are Like _____* at the top of a sheet of chart paper. Below them, write the word *popcorn*. Ask and have the students think quietly to themselves about:

Q *What are words like to you?*

Call on just a couple of students to share their thinking with the class, and record their ideas on the chart. Without sharing too many ideas, have the students open to the next blank page in their notebooks and list more ideas for what words are like.

After about 5 minutes, signal for the students' attention and have volunteers share their thinking with the class. Continue to add their ideas to the "Words Are Like" chart.

◀ **Teacher Note**

If the students have difficulty generating ideas, suggest some like those in the diagram below; then ask, "What other ideas do you have?"

Words Are Like _____.

- popcorn
- ants marching across the page
- puzzle pieces
- birds that fly through your mind
- letters that dance together
- blobs of paint

Explain that during writing time today, the students will continue to write poems. Tell them that you will end the writing time a little early to give pairs a chance to share their writing.

Briefly review the "Notes About Poems" chart and encourage the students to refer to the chart as they write today.

WRITING TIME

Teacher Note

You may want to shorten today's
writing time to leave more time
for the pair conferences in Step 5. ▶

4 ▶ **Write Independently**

Have the students return to their seats and write poems silently for
20–30 minutes. Join them in writing for a few minutes; then confer
with individual students.

> ## TEACHER CONFERENCE NOTE
>
> Continue to confer individually with your students about the
> poems they are writing. Ask each student to show you a draft
> of a poem and to read it aloud to you. Ask yourself:
>
> - Is this student attempting to write a poem rather than
>   a story?
>
> - Does she include sensory details?
>
> - What other elements of poetry does she try to include
>   in his poem?
>
> Support students by asking them questions such as:
>
> **Q** *What is this poem about?*
>
> **Q** *What sensory details [are you including/can you include]?
>   How will that help your reader imagine what's happening?*
>
> **Q** *Tell me about the lines and stanzas in your poem.*
>
> **Q** *What sounds are you thinking about as you write your poem?*
>
> **Q** *Where might you use repetition? How might that help
>   your reader understand your poem? What other sounds
>   are you including?*
>
> Document your observations for each student on the
> "Conference Notes" record sheet (BLM1).

Signal to let the students know when writing time is over.

SHARING AND REFLECTING

5 ▸ Confer in Pairs About Poems

Gather the class with partners sitting together, facing you. Explain that each student will choose a poem to read to his partner today and that you would like partners to close their eyes and try to get a picture in their mind as they listen to each other's poems. After hearing the poem, they will tell their partner what they imagined as they listened. Ask:

Q *How will you read your poem so your partner is able to get a mental picture?*

Q *What kinds of things will you listen for to help you get a mental picture?*

> **Students might say:**
>
> "I will read my poem slowly so my partner can think about the words."
>
> "I will listen for sensory details, like what things look like or sound like."

Encourage the students to read their poems aloud more than once, if necessary. Have partners share their writing with each other.

Observe the students closely and provide sufficient time for both partners to share their poems before signaling for their attention.

Reflect on Pair Conferences and Poems

Help the students reflect on their work today by asking:

Q *What mental images did you get as you listened to your partner's poems today?*

Q *What did you do to show interest in your partner's writing?*

Remind the students that they will each choose one poem next week to revise and publish in a class book.

◀ **Teacher Note**

If necessary, signal the students about halfway through sharing time so partners can switch roles if they have not yet done so.

flamingo
by Valerie Worth

The
Flamingo
Lingers
A
Long
Time
Over
One
Pink
Leg;

Later
He
Ponders
Upon
The
Other
For
A
While
Instead.

Poetry

crickets

by Valerie Worth

Crickets
Talk
In the tall
Grass
All
Late summer
Long.
When
Summer
Is gone,
The dry
Grass
Whispers
Alone.

Windshield Wiper

by Eve Merriam

fog smog   fog smog
tissue paper   tissue paper
clear the blear clear the smear

fog more   fog more
splat splat   down pour
rubber scraper   rubber scraper
overshoes   macintosh
bumbershoot   muddle on
slosh through   slosh through

drying up   drying up
sky lighter   sky lighter
nearly clear   nearly clear
clearing clearing veer
clear here clear

from The Bells
by Edgar Allan Poe

Hear the sledges with the bells —
Silver bells!
What a world of merriment their melody foretells!
How they tinkle, tinkle, tinkle,
In the icy air of night!
While the stars that oversprinkle
All the heavens seems to twinkle
With a crystalline delight;
Keeping time, time, time,
In a sort of Runic rhyme,
To the tintinnabulation that so musically wells
From the bells, bells, bells, bells,
Bells, bells, bells —
From the jingling and the tinkling of the bells.

Poetry

I Love the Look of Words
by Maya Angelou

Popcorn leaps, popping from the floor
of a hot black skillet
and into my mouth.
Black words leap
snapping from the white
page. Rushing into my eyes. Sliding
into my brain which gobbles them
the way my tongue and teeth
chomp the buttered popcorn.

When I have stopped reading,
ideas from the words stay stuck
in my mind, like the sweet
smell of butter perfuming my
fingers long after the popcorn
is finished.

I love the book and the look of words
the weight of ideas that popped into my mind
I love the tracks
of new thinking in my mind.

Week 3 Overview

GENRE: POETRY

Writing Focus

- Students review their poetry drafts and select one to revise, proofread, and publish.

- Students revise their poems thinking about imagery, sound, and form.

- Students explore intentionally breaking punctuation rules in poetry.

- Students proofread and publish their writing.

- Students confer with one another and the teacher.

Social Focus

- Students act in fair and caring ways.

- Students listen to the thinking of others and share their own.

- Students express interest in and appreciation for one another's writing.

DO AHEAD

- (Optional) If computers are available, consider having the students type and print their poems. You might also recruit parent volunteers to help them.

TEACHER AS WRITER

"I believe every space and comma is a living part of the poem and has its function, just as every muscle and pore of the body has its function. And the way the lines are broken is a functioning part essential to the life of the poem."
— *Denise Levertov*

Reread the poems you wrote last week and think about "every space and comma" and "the way the lines are broken." Try rewriting a poem by breaking the lines in other places, adding spaces, or adding or deleting punctuation. Ask yourself how the poem changes as you try these variations.

Day 1

Materials

- "Notes About Poetry" chart
- Pad of small self-stick notes for each student
- *Assessment Resource Book*

Selecting and Revising Drafts

In this lesson, the students:

- Review their poetry drafts and select one to develop and publish
- Reread their writing critically
- Analyze and revise for sensory details, sounds, form, and imagery
- Ask one another questions about their writing

GETTING READY TO WRITE

1▶ Review Poetry

Gather the class with partners sitting together, facing you. Have the students bring their notebooks and pencils with them. Review that over the past two weeks the students have been writing drafts of poems. Ask:

Q *What have you learned about what makes a poem a poem?*

Direct the students' attention to the "Notes About Poems" chart and review the items on it.

Explain that today the students will review all of their poetry drafts and select one to develop for publication in a class book.

2▶ Review and Select Drafts

Teacher Note

If the students have difficulty answering this question, offer some ideas like those in the "Students might say" note and ask, "What else might you look for?"

Ask and briefly discuss:

Q *As you're looking through your poems, what might you want to look for to help you decide on one to develop?*

Students might say:

"I want to look for a poem that has some good sensory details."

"I wrote some poems with interesting sounds. I think I'll pick one of those."

"I want my poem to be different from everyone else's, so I'm going to look for one that is unique."

Give the students a few minutes to review and select their poems. If they finish, have them select a second poem to develop if they have time.

3 Facilitate Guided Rereading of Drafts

Have the students return to their seats and open their notebooks to the draft they selected. Explain that the students will carefully reread the draft, and that you will help them think about ways they can add to, revise, and improve their poem. Have them quietly reread their draft and look up when they are finished.

Distribute a pad of self-stick notes to each student. Explain that you will ask the students to look for and think about several specific things in their draft.

Say the following prompt and give the students several minutes to review their draft and mark passages with self-stick notes:

● *Find one place in your poem where you describe, or could describe, something using sensory details. Mark the margin next to that place with a self-stick note and write "sensory details" on it.*

When most students have finished, signal for their attention and ask several volunteers to read what they marked. Probe their thinking by asking questions such as:

Q *What do you hope your reader will imagine when reading that line?*

Using the same procedure, take the students through the following prompts, saying them one at a time and giving the students time to mark passages before having volunteers share.

◀ **Teacher Note**

The purpose of this guided rereading is to give the students experience with critically reading and thinking about their drafts *before* beginning to revise. Note that some students will not be finished with their poems and will need time this week to both complete and revise them.

Teacher Note

◀ If students have difficulty finding and marking sensory details, make the prompt more specific by saying:

● Mark a place where you describe, or could describe, what something looks like.

● Mark a place where you describe, or could describe, what something sounds like.

● Mark a place where you describe, or could describe, what something smells or tastes like.

● Mark a place where you describe, or could describe, what something feels like.

- *Do the sounds of the words in your poem help to communicate what the poem is about? Find a place where you might be able to add some interesting-sounding words. Mark it with a self-stick note and write "sounds" on it.*

- *Do you have stanzas in your poem? If so, do you have the same number of lines in each stanza? If not, mark this with a self-stick note so you can decide if you want to give all of the stanzas the same number of lines. Write "number of lines" on the note.*

- *Does your poem have a particular shape? If so, does the shape help to communicate what your poem is about? If you think you can change the shape to better communicate what your poem is about, put a self-stick note on the edge of your page and write "shape" on it.*

WRITING TIME

 Reread and Revise Poems

Write the following tasks on the board and have the students write silently for 20–30 minutes.

- Review the things you marked with self-stick notes.

- Revise your poem.

- Remove the self-stick notes when you finish revising.

- If necessary, continue adding to your poem until it is finished.

If the students finish, they may follow the same procedure to review and revise a second poem. Join the students in writing for a few minutes; then walk around the class and observe.

CLASS ASSESSMENT NOTE

As the students revise their poems, observe and ask yourself:

- Are the students able to revise their drafts to include sensory details and/or sounds?

- Are they thinking about what their poem looks like on the page?

- Do they seem engaged in revising their poems?

Support students who are having difficulty by asking them questions such as:

Q *What were you thinking about when you marked this place on your draft?*

Q *What words could you add to help the reader [see/hear/ smell/taste/feel] what you're writing about?*

Q *Read your poem aloud. What sounds do you hear? Do those sounds help to communicate what your poem is about? If not, what words might have the sounds that would make sense in your poem?*

Q *What do you want your poem to look like on the page? How can you arrange the words so it looks like that?*

Record your observations in the *Assessment Resource Book*.

Signal to let the students know when writing time is over.

SHARING AND REFLECTING

Reflect on Revisions and Creativity

Have the students review their revisions from today and choose one revised line to share with the class. Encourage them to choose a line that they feel is an improvement over the original line and that shows their creativity. After a moment, go around the room and have each student read his line aloud, without comment.

After the students have read their lines, facilitate discussion among the students by asking:

Q *How does the line you read improve your poem?*

Q *What lines did you hear your classmates read that got your imagination going?*

Q *What questions do you want to ask a classmate about his or her writing?*

Explain that the students will proofread and begin writing final versions of their poems tomorrow.

Day 2

Proofreading

In this lesson, the students:

- Explore how poets follow and break punctuation rules
- Decide how they will punctuate their poems
- Proofread and correct spelling and punctuation
- Begin writing the final version of their poems

GETTING READY TO WRITE

1 ▶ Discuss How Poets Follow and Break Rules

Have partners sit together at desks today. Explain that today they will work on the final version of their poem. They will publish it later in the week by sharing it from the Author's Chair and contributing it to a book for the class library.

Explain that today the students will proofread their poems for spelling errors and make sure they have punctuated their poems exactly the way they want to. Point out that poets don't always follow the rules when it comes to punctuation. However, when they break the rules, they do so on purpose, not accidentally. Explain that today the students will look at how poets follow and break the rules; then they will look at their own poems and decide how to punctuate them. Ask:

Q   *When writing sentences, what do we usually do at the beginning and end to make sure they are written correctly?*

If necessary, remind the students that sentences begin with a capital letter and end with a period, question mark, or exclamation point.

Materials

- Transparency of "Child Frightened by a Thunderstorm" (BLM30)
- Transparency of "flamingo" (BLM31)
- Transparency of "Windshield Wiper" (BLM32)
- Transparency of "I Love the Look of Words" (BLM33)
- *Student Writing Handbook* pages 39, 41
- Supply of loose, lined paper for final versions
- (Optional) Computers for word processing (see "Do Ahead" on page 605)

Show the transparency of "Child Frightened by a Thunderstorm" and have the students turn to this poem on *Student Writing Handbook* page 39. Ask them to scan the poem to see if the poet follows the rules for punctuating sentences. After a moment, ask:

Q *Does he follow the rules in this poem? How do you know?*

As the students refer to punctuation in the poem, underline or circle the punctuation marks on the transparency. If necessary, point out that this poet follows the rules by capitalizing the first letter in each of the four sentences in the poem and ending the sentences with periods.

Next, show the transparency of "flamingo" and ask the students to turn to this poem on handbook page 41. Ask:

 Q *What do you notice about how this poem is punctuated? Turn to your partner.*

Have a few volunteers share with the class. If necessary, point out that this poet intentionally breaks the rules by capitalizing not just the first letter of the sentence but all the words in the poem. In addition, she does not capitalize the title.

Repeat this procedure for "Windshield Wiper" and "I Love the Look of Words," drawing the students' attention to the last stanza in "I Love the Look of Words." Use the transparencies to mark places the students refer to as they share.

2 Review Drafts for Punctuation

Ask the students to review their poems and think quietly to themselves about the following questions:

Q *Do you follow the rule of capitalizing the first letters of sentences and using periods at the ends? If so, do you do this all the way through your poem?*

Q *If you did not start out following this rule, what did you do instead? Do you want to leave it this way or revise it to follow the rules?*

Teacher Note ▶

If necessary, point out that, while "Windshield Wiper" has no punctuation at all, "I Love the Look of Words" begins with standard sentence punctuation but ends with missing punctuation in the last stanza. If there's time, you might ask:

Q *Why do you think Maya Angelou chose to leave out the punctuation in the last stanza?*

Your students may have difficulty answering this question. One idea is that the words in the last stanza are treated more like popcorn piled into a bowl than parts of sentences.

Q *If you choose not to follow the rules, do you do this consistently all the way through your poem?*

Give the students a few moments to check and revise their punctuation and capitalization, and encourage them to use the poems in their *Student Writing Handbooks* as models for how to punctuate their own poems, if they wish.

3 Briefly Review Proofreading for Spelling and Conventions

Remind the students that, in addition to checking their sentence punctuation and capitalization, they should use their word bank and proofreading notes to help them proofread their drafts before publishing (these components were introduced in Unit 2, Week 3, Days 1 and 2; see pages 128–135). Briefly review these procedures by reminding the students to:

- Circle words in their drafts that they are unsure how to spell, and look the words up in their word bank. They will add to their word bank any words that are not already there after looking up their correct spelling in a dictionary or other source.

- Use their proofreading notes as a list of things to check before publishing. The students will correct any errors by crossing out the error and writing the correction next to it (unless, for some reason, they choose to intentionally break the rule).

WRITING TIME

Proofread Drafts and Write Final Versions

Have the students work on proofreading their poems. Provide lined paper to students who finish proofreading and are ready to begin their final versions. As they work, circulate, observe, and offer assistance. When students seem to be working independently, confer with individual students.

◀ **Teacher Note**

To provide your students with practice with the skills and conventions of written English, do the appropriate activities in the *Skill Practice Teaching Guide* with them.

TEACHER CONFERENCE NOTE

Continue to confer individually with your students about the poems they are writing. Ask each student to show you a draft of a poem and to read it aloud to you. Ask yourself:

* Is this student attempting to write a poem rather than a story?

* Does he include sensory details?

* What other elements of poetry does he try to include in his poem?

Support students by asking them questions such as:

Q *What is this poem about?*

Q *What sensory details [are you including/can you include]? How will that help your reader imagine what's happening?*

Q *Where might you use repetition? How might that help your reader understand your poem? What other sounds are you including?*

Q *How have you decided to punctuate your poem? If you decided to follow the rules, are you doing this all the way through your poem? If not, what are you doing instead?*

Document your observations for each student on the "Conference Notes" record sheet (BLM1).

Signal to let the students know when writing time is over.

SHARING AND REFLECTING

 Reflect on Proofreading

Ask and briefly discuss:

Q *What words did you find in your word bank today? How did you check on words that were not in the word bank?*

Q *What corrections did you make in your draft after reviewing your proofreading notes?*

Explain that the students will finish working on their final versions tomorrow.

Day 3

Materials

- Supply of lined paper for final versions
- "Notes About Poems" chart
- (Optional) Computers for word processing
- Chair to use for Author's Chair sharing

Publishing

In this lesson, the students:

- Write the final version of their poems
- Present their poems from the Author's Chair
- Express interest in and appreciation for one another's writing
- Ask one another questions about their writing

GETTING READY TO WRITE

1▶ Briefly Review Poetry

Have the students stay in their seats. Explain that today they will finish working on the final version of their poems. Students who finish will begin sharing their pieces from the Author's Chair after the writing time.

Direct the students' attention to the "Notes About Poems" chart and review the items on it. Encourage them to keep these things in mind as they write the final version of their poems today.

WRITING TIME

 ### 2▶ Finish Final Versions of Poems

Have the students work on finishing their final versions. If they finish, they may proofread and write the final version of a second poem. When they seem to be working independently, confer with individual students.

TEACHER CONFERENCE NOTE

Continue to confer individually with your students about the poems they are writing. Ask each student to show you a draft of a poem and to read it aloud to you. Ask yourself:

- Is this student attempting to write a poem rather than a story?

- Does she include sensory details?

- What other elements of poetry does she try to include in this poem?

Support students by asking them questions such as:

Q *What is this poem about?*

Q *What sensory details [are you including/can you include]? How will that help your reader imagine what's happening?*

Q *Where might you use repetition? How might that help your reader understand your poem? What other sounds are you including?*

Q *How have you decided to punctuate your poem? If you decided to follow the rules, are you doing this all the way through your poem? If not, what are you doing instead?*

Document your observations for each student on the "Conference Notes" record sheet (BLM1).

Signal to let the students know when writing time is over.

SHARING AND REFLECTING

Review Sharing from the Author's Chair

Gather the class with partners sitting together, facing the Author's Chair. Remind the students of the procedure you established for presenting writing from the Author's Chair (see Unit 2, Week 3, Day 4, pages 142–144).

Before asking students to share from the Author's Chair today, discuss how they will act, both as presenting authors and as members of the audience. Ask and discuss:

Q *How will you let the author know that you're interested in his or her poem? Why is it important to express interest in one another's writing?*

Direct the students' attention to the "Notes About Poems" chart and review the items on it. Encourage them to listen for things that appear on the chart as they hear one another's poems.

4 ▶ Conduct Author's Chair Sharing

Ask a student who has finished the final version of her poem to read it aloud twice, slowly and clearly, from the Author's Chair. At the end of the sharing, facilitate a discussion using questions like those that follow, and give the author an opportunity to respond to the class's comments and questions.

Q *What did you imagine as you listened to [Rashidah's] poem?*

Q *What did you enjoy about hearing [Rashidah's] poem?*

Q (Refer to the "Notes About Poems" chart.) *What items on the "Notes About Poems" chart did you notice in [Rashidah's] poem?*

Q *What questions can we ask [Rashidah] about her poem?*

Repeat this procedure to have other students share from the Author's Chair.

5 ▶ Reflect on Audience Behavior During Author's Chair Sharing

Ask and briefly discuss:

Q *What did we do well as an audience today? What might we want to work on the next time poets share their work?*

Q *If you shared a poem today, did you feel that people were interested in and appreciative of your efforts? Why or why not?*

Explain that all of the students will get a chance to share their poems from the Author's Chair in the coming days.

Day 4

Materials

- "Poet Quotes: What Is Poetry?" (page 625)
- *Student Writing Handbook* page 46
- Supply of lined paper for final versions
- (Optional) Computers for word processing
- Chair to use for Author's Chair sharing
- "Notes About Poems" chart

Publishing

In this lesson, the students:

- Think about the question, "What is poetry?"
- Finish writing the final version of their poems
- Present their poem from the Author's Chair
- Express interest in and appreciation for one another's writing
- Ask one another questions about their writing

GETTING READY TO WRITE

 Think About "What Is Poetry?"

Gather the class with partners sitting together, facing you. Have the students bring their *Student Writing Handbooks* with them. Remind them that they began this unit by considering the question, "What makes a poem a poem?" Tell them that many professional poets have tried to answer a similar question: "What is poetry?"

Ask the students to open to *Student Writing Handbook* page 46 and follow along as you read some poets' definitions of poetry aloud (see your copy on page 625 of the *Teacher's Manual*). Invite the students to think as they listen about what their own definition of poetry might be.

Read "Poet Quotes: What Is Poetry?" aloud, slowly and clearly. Clarify vocabulary as you read.

> ### Suggested Vocabulary
>
> **distilled:** concentrated and pure
> **distorted:** twisted, ugly

Ask and briefly discuss:

Q *What do you think about as you read these poets' definitions of poetry?*

Q *What definitions do you agree with? Disagree with? Why?*

Use "Think, Pair, Share" to have partners first think about, then discuss:

Q *How would you answer the question, "What is poetry?"* [pause] *Turn to your partner.*

After partners have had a chance to share, have a few volunteers share their thinking with the class.

Explain that each poet has his or her own ideas about what poetry is. Invite the students to continue to think about this question as they finish writing their final versions today. If they have already finished, tell them that you would like them to spend time writing some of their own definitions for poetry in their notebooks during writing time today. They will have a chance to share these with the class.

WRITING TIME

Finish Final Versions of Poems

Have the students return to their seats and work on finishing their final versions. If they finish, have them write some of their own definitions for poetry in their notebooks. When they seem to be working independently, confer with individual students.

FACILITATION TIP

Reflect on your experience over the past three weeks with **responding neutrally with interest** during class discussions. Does this practice feel natural to you? Are you integrating it into class discussions throughout the school day? What effect is it having on the students? We encourage you to continue to try this practice and reflect on students' responses as you facilitate class discussions in the future.

TEACHER CONFERENCE NOTE

Continue to confer individually with your students about the poems they are writing. Ask each student to show you a draft of a poem and to read it aloud to you. Ask yourself:

- Is this student attempting to write a poem rather than a story?

- Does he include sensory details?

- What other elements of poetry does he try to include in his poem?

Support students by asking them questions such as:

Q *What is this poem about?*

Q *What sensory details [are you including/can you include]? How will that help your reader imagine what's happening?*

Q *Where might you use repetition? How might that help your reader understand your poem? What other sounds are you including?*

Q *How have you decided to punctuate your poem? If you decided to follow the rules, are you doing this all the way through your poem? If not, what are you doing instead?*

Document your observations for each student on the "Conference Notes" record sheet (BLM1).

Signal to let the students know when writing time is over. Before moving to Author's Chair sharing, ask and briefly discuss:

Q *What definitions for poetry did you write today? Read them to us.*

SHARING AND REFLECTING

 Prepare for Author's Chair Sharing

Gather the class with partners sitting together, facing the Author's Chair. Remind the students of the procedure you established for presenting writing from the Author's Chair. Encourage them to thin as they listen to one another's poems about things they recognize from the "Notes About Poems" chart.

4 ## Conduct Author's Chair Sharing

Have a student read his poem aloud twice, slowly and clearly, from the Author's Chair. At the end of the sharing, facilitate a discussion using questions like those that follow, and give the author an opportunity to respond to the class's comments and questions.

Q *What did you imagine as you listened to [Octavio's] poem?*

Q *What did you enjoy about hearing [Octavio's] poem?*

Q (Refer to the "Notes About Poems" chart.) *What items on the "Notes About Poems" chart did you notice in [Octavio's] poem?*

Q *What questions can we ask [Octavio] about his poem?*

Repeat this procedure to have other students share from the Author's Chair.

Reflect on Audience Behavior During Author's Chair Sharing

Ask and briefly discuss:

Q *What did we do well as an audience today? What do we still want to work on the next time poets share their work?*

Q *If you shared a poem today, did you feel that people were interested in and appreciative of your efforts? Why or why not?*

Assure the students that they will all get to share their published poems from the Author's Chair in the coming days. After the poems are read aloud, assemble the poems in a class book, and place the book in the class library so students can read it during independent reading time.

Remind the students that poets, like all writers, become better over time as they practice writing more and more. Encourage students who feel drawn to poetry to continue to write poems during their free time and during the open weeks of this program.

Teacher Note

If necessary, repeat the "Sharing and Reflecting" section of today's lesson for a few more days, or even another week, to give all of the students time to finish publishing their poems (see Open Weeks in the front matter on page xvi). Students who finish may begin a new piece of writing (poetry or otherwise) or continue working on any piece of writing they started earlier.

Even if you decide to begin another genre unit immediately, continue to have the students share their poems from the Author's Chair until everyone has had a chance to do so.

Teacher Note

This is the last week of the unit. You will need to reassign partners before beginning the next unit.

EXTENSION

Write Letters Home About Poetry

Provide letter-writing practice for the students by having them write a letter home about what they learned about writing poetry. Stimulate their thinking by reviewing the "Notes About Poems" chart and discussing questions such as:

Q *What makes a poem a poem?*

Q *What else did you learn about writing poetry?*

Q *What steps did you go through to develop and publish your own poem?*

If necessary, review the elements of a letter (date, salutation, body, closing, and signature) by modeling or writing a shared sample letter with the class. Have the students write and proofread their letters; then attach each student's letter to a copy of her published poem and send it home.

Poet Quotes: What Is Poetry?

"Poetry is the spontaneous overflow of powerful feelings."

— William Wordsworth

"Poetry is language at its most distilled and most powerful."

— Rita Dove

"Poetry is a mirror which makes beautiful [what] is distorted."

— Percy Bysshe Shelley

"Poetry is an echo, asking a shadow to dance."

— Carl Sandburg

"Poetry is the art of creating imaginary gardens with real toads."

— Marianne Moore

Revisiting the Writing Community

Revisiting the Writing Community

Unit 8

Revisiting the Writing Community

During this one-week unit, the students review the writing they have done this year and reflect on their growth as writers and as members of the classroom writing community. They plan their summer writing and write letters to next year's class about what it means to be a writer. They thank their classmates for supporting them this year, and they express interest in and appreciation for one another's writing and thinking.

UNIT OVERVIEW

WEEK	DAY 1	DAY 2	DAY 3	DAY 4
1	**Reflecting on Writing** **Focus:** Reflect on growth as writers	**Reflecting on Writing** **Focus:** Write to next year's class about how to be a good writer	**Planning for Writing** **Focus:** Plan summer writing	**Reflecting on Community** **Focus:** Reflect on growth as community members; thank classmates

Week 1 Overview

UNIT 8: REVISITING THE WRITING COMMUNITY

Writing Focus

- Students review their writing from the year.

- Students reflect on their growth as writers.

- Students write to next year's class about how to be a good writer.

- Students plan their summer writing.

Social Focus

- Students build the writing community.

- Students act in fair and caring ways.

- Students build on one another's thinking.

- Students express interest in and appreciation for one another's writing.

DO AHEAD

- Prior to Day 1, gather all the students' published writing from the classroom library, including individual pieces, pair work, and class books. Return each student's work to him or her, disassembling class books. You might copy pair work and have partners decide who will take the original and who will take the copy. If necessary, provide folders so the students can keep all of their pieces together.

TEACHER AS WRITER

"Your first duty as a writer is to write to please yourself. And you have no duty towards anyone else."

— *Iris Chang*

This week take some time to look over the writing you have done this year in your writing notebook. Compare the first few pieces you wrote to your latest pieces. What do you notice about how you have changed or grown as a writer? What challenges did you grapple with? How has your attitude about yourself as a writer changed? What do you hope for your writing practice in the coming year? Write and date your reflections in your writing notebook.

Day 1

Materials

- Students' published writing, returned to them (see "Do Ahead" on page 629)
- Pad of small, self-stick notes for each student
- "Conference Notes" record sheet for each student (BLM1)
- *Assessment Resource Book*

Teacher Note

You will not assign new partners for this week. Either have the students work with their partner from the previous unit or simply have them turn and talk to someone sitting near them during "Turn to Your Partner."

Teacher Note

This lesson may require an extended class period.

Reflecting on Writing

In this lesson, the students:

- Review their writing from the year
- Reflect and write about how they have grown as writers
- Think about challenges they faced and what they have learned about writing
- Listen to the thinking of others and share their own
- Express interest in and appreciation for one another's writing

GETTING READY TO WRITE

 Discuss Goals for the Week

Have the students stay at their desks for the lesson today. Have them get their writing notebooks, published writing from the year, and pencils.

Explain that during this last week of the *Being a Writer* program, the students will review the writing they did this year, think about how they have changed and grown as writers and as members of a writing community, reflect and write about what they have learned about good writing, and plan their summer writing.

2 **Review Published Writing from the Year**

Distribute a pad of self-stick notes to each student and explain that they will first look through their published pieces from the year. Write the following questions on the board and tell the students that you would like them to think about the questions as they review their pieces.

> - What is one of the best published pieces of writing you have done this year? Mark it with the word "Best" on a self-stick note.
>
> - What piece of writing did you have the most fun working on this year? Mark it with the word "Fun" on a self-stick note.
>
> - What piece of writing was the most challenging for you? Mark it with the word "Challenging" on a self-stick note.

Point out that the students might decide to put multiple self-stick notes on a single piece of writing.

Give the students ample time to look through their published pieces and mark them with self-stick notes. When most students have marked their best, most fun, and most challenging pieces, signal for attention. Have them separate out the marked pieces of writing and put their other published pieces away.

Review Notebook Writing

Explain that for each of the flagged pieces, the students should find the drafts they wrote for those pieces in their notebooks and mark them with self-stick notes. Tell them you would like them to reread those drafts and try to remember what it was like to write them.

Give the students ample time to review their notebooks. Then signal for their attention.

Share Marked Pieces with Another Student

Explain that the students will share their thinking about the three pieces of writing they marked with another student sitting near them. Encourage them to tell each other what they remember about working on each piece and why they chose those three as their best, most fun, and most challenging.

As partners share, walk around, listen, and observe.

> ## CLASS ASSESSMENT NOTE
>
> Listen to students as they share in pairs and ask yourself:
>
> * Are the students able to explain why they marked a piece as their best, most fun, or most challenging?
>
> * Do they refer to their first drafts or other steps in the writing process in talking about their pieces?
>
> * Do they listen carefully to each other?
>
> Record your observations in the *Assessment Resource Book*.

After allowing enough time for both partners to share their writing, signal for the students' attention. Have a few volunteers tell the class about one piece of writing they marked and share what they thought about it.

 5   Get Ready to Write About Growth as Writers

Ask the students to look at the first couple of drafts they wrote in their notebooks and to compare them to the last few drafts they wrote. After a moment, ask the students to think to themselves as they listen to the following questions. Ask the questions one at a time, pausing between each question to give the students time to think.

Q   *What do you notice about the way you wrote at the beginning of the year, compared to the way you write now?*

Q   *What kinds of words did you use in your early pieces, compared to your more recent pieces?*

Q   *How do you think you have changed as a writer this year?*

Without sharing as a class, explain that you would like the students to open to the next blank page in their notebooks and write their reflections about how they think they have grown or changed as a writer this year, based on looking at their work from both the beginning and the end of the year. They do not need to write answers for each question you have asked.

WRITING TIME

6 Write Reflections About Growth as Writers

Have the students write their reflections silently for 10–20 minutes. If they finish, they may write about anything they choose.

TEACHER CONFERENCE NOTE

You may wish to confer once more with individual students this week, using their three marked pieces of writing as the topic of the conference. Have each student show you the pieces she flagged as her best, most fun, and most challenging and tell you what she remembers about working on those pieces and why she flagged them.

Document your observations for each student on the "Conferent Notes" record sheet. Use the "Conference Notes" record sheets during conferences throughout this week (BLM1).

Signal to let the students know when writing time is over.

SHARING AND REFLECTING

Share Reflections

Ask the students to reread what they wrote today and underline a sentence that tells one way they think they have grown or changed as a writer this year. Give them a moment to select their sentence, and then go around the room and have each student read his sentence aloud to the class, without comment.

When all the students have read their sentence about how they have grown or changed, ask and briefly discuss as a class:

Q *What did you hear about how your classmates have grown as writers this year?*

Q *What questions do you want to ask a classmate about the sentence he or she shared?*

Explain that tomorrow the students will continue to reflect on how they have grown and what they have learned as writers.

Day 2

Reflecting on Writing

In this lesson, the students:

* Write to next year's class about ways to be a good writer
* Get ideas by listening to others

GETTING READY TO WRITE

1 Review Genres Explored This Year

Have the students stay at their desks today. Remind them that they reflected yesterday on how they have changed or grown as writers over the past year. Point out that they have learned a lot about how to be good writers of personal narratives, fiction stories, nonfiction informational pieces, persuasive essays, and poetry.

Explain that today the students will reflect on what they have learned about how to be a good writer. Then they will write letters to next year's fifth grade class to help them become good writers.

Reflect on Ways to Be a Good Writer

Use "Think, Pair, Share" to have the students first think about and then discuss:

Q *What have you learned about how to be a good writer?* [pause] *Turn to your partner.*

After the students have talked in pairs, signal for their attention and have volunteers report their thinking to the class. As they share, record their ideas on a sheet of chart paper entitled, "Ways to Be a Good Writer."

Materials

* *Student Writing Handbooks*
* Chart paper and a marker
* Loose, lined paper for writing letters
* *Assessment Resource Book*

◀ **Teacher Note**

If the students have difficulty generating ideas for this question, suggest some ideas like those in the "Students might say" note. Then ask, "What else have you learned about how to be a good writer?"

Students might say:

"I learned that good writers often use sensory details to help the reader imagine what's happening."

"I learned that to be a good writer you have to make sure your writing makes sense to people."

"To be a good writer, you have to be able to think about things and revise your writing so it gets better."

"I learned that writers become good because they practice writing all the time."

"I learned that good writers write about things that interest them."

Ways to Be a Good Writer

- Use sensory details.

- Check to see if it makes sense.

- Revise to improve your writing.

- Practice writing all the time.

- Write about what interests you.

Explain that during writing time today, the students will each write a letter to next year's fifth grade class, giving them some advice to help them become good writers. Tell them that they may include things listed on the chart as well as other ideas they have. Point out that the letters should be written in their own words and should be friendly and encouraging in tone.

If necessary, write the date and a salutation (for example, "Dear Next Year's Fifth Graders") where everyone can see it so that the students can copy these if they need to. Also remind them to sign their name at the bottom of their letters when they finish.

WRITING TIME

3 Independently Write Letters to Next Year's Class

Distribute loose, lined paper and have the students write their letters for 20–30 minutes. If they finish, have them proofread their letters for spelling and punctuation using the word bank and proofreading notes sections of their *Student Writing Handbooks.*

As the students work, walk around the room and observe them.

> **CLASS ASSESSMENT NOTE**
>
> Observe the students and ask yourself:
>
> - Do the students write confidently about ways to be a good writer?
>
> - Do students who seemed cautious or inhibited about their writing early in the year write more freely now?
>
> - Do they confidently use the word bank and proofreading notes to proofread their writing?
>
> Record your observations in the *Assessment Resource Book.*

Signal to let the students know when writing time is over.

SHARING AND REFLECTING

Share Letters and Reflect on Work Together

Have the students share their letters with someone sitting next to them. Remind them to listen carefully to their partner's letter so they can share what their partner wrote with the class.

After giving some time for students to share, signal for their attention and discuss:

Q *What advice did your partner include in his letter to next year's class?*

Q *Is your partner's letter friendly and encouraging? What does she write to make it feel that way?*

Q *What did you do to help your work with your partner go well today?*

Teacher Note

If necessary, give the students time to finish writing and proofreading their letters, then collect them into a binder to share with your incoming class this fall.

Day 3

Materials

- "Writing Habits of Professional Authors" (see page 644)

- A highlighter or marker for each student

Planning for Writing

In this lesson, the students:

- Learn about the writing habits of professional authors
- Plan their summer writing
- Get ideas by listening to others
- Express interest in and appreciation for one another's writing

GETTING READY TO WRITE

 Generate Topics to Write About over the Summer

Have the students stay at their desks today. Review that they have been looking back over the year and thinking about what they have learned and how they have grown as writers this year. Tell them that today they will look forward and think about how they plan to keep writing over the summer.

Ask the students to open to the writing ideas section of their writing notebooks and to review the ideas they wrote over the year. After sufficient time for the students to review their ideas, ask:

 Q *What are some ideas you didn't get a chance to write about this year that you are still interested in writing about? Turn and talk to someone sitting next to you.*

Distribute a highlighter or marker to each student and explain that you would like them to highlight or mark ideas in their notebooks that they are still interested in writing about. After they have had a chance to highlight their ideas, ask them to turn to a clean page and spend a few more minutes brainstorming and listing other ideas they might want to write about this summer.

After a moment, ask and discuss as a class:

Q   *What are some things you might want to write about this summer?*

Q   *Why is it important for you to keep writing on your own this summer?*

> **Students might say:**
>
> "It's important to keep writing on our own so we don't forget
> how to be good writers over the summer."
>
> "It's important to keep writing so we can keep getting better
> at writing."
>
> "In addition to what [Ansel] said, it's important to keep writing
> because it's fun!"

Point out that most professional authors have daily habits that help
them keep writing. They have a special time and place in which they
write, and they write for a certain length of time. Sometimes they use
particular materials, like a certain pen or kind of paper. Explain that
today you will read some quotes by professional authors about their
writing habits. The students will then think about what kinds of habits
they want to have to help them keep writing over the summer.

Read and Discuss Some Professional Authors' Writing Habits

Read "Writing Habits of Professional Authors" aloud slowly and
clearly, clarifying vocabulary as you read.

> **Suggested Vocabulary**
>
> **cubicle:** a small work area
> **lull:** short, quiet break
> **teak:** a kind of wood

Ask and briefly discuss:

Q   *What habits did you hear about?*

Q   *What ideas did this give you about habits you can set for yourself
at home to help you keep writing this summer?* ▶

Explain that during writing time today, you would like the students to write in their notebooks about what they will do to help them continue to write this summer. Encourage them to write specific habits they want to establish, such as where, when, how often, and how long they will write each day. Also invite them to think about what objects they would like to have around them to help them write.

If the students finish, they may add to their list of topics to write about this summer or choose one of those ideas and write about it.

WRITING TIME

 ### Write Independently About Writing Habits

Write the following directions on the board and have the students work quietly for 20–30 minutes.

- Write about what you will do to help yourself continue writing this summer.

- Add to your list of topics to write about over the summer.

- Pick one of your summer topics and start writing about it.

As the students work, walk around and observe or continue to confer with individual students (see the Teacher Conference Note on Day 1, page 633).

Signal to let the students know when writing time is over.

SHARING AND REFLECTING

 ### Share Plans for Summer Writing

Ask the students to reread what they wrote today and underline a sentence that tells one thing they will do to help them keep writing this summer. Give them a moment to select their sentence. Then go around the room and have each student read her sentence aloud to the class, without comment.

When all the students have read their sentence, ask and briefly discuss as a class:

Q *What ideas did you hear that you want to add to your list?*

Q *What questions do you want to ask a classmate about the sentence he or she shared?*

Give the students a moment to add ideas to their lists, if they wish. Encourage them to continue writing as much as they can this summer and to focus on enjoying their own writing.

Day 4

Reflecting on Community

In this lesson, the students:

- Reflect on their contributions to the writing community
- Reflect on how they have benefited from the writing community
- Thank one another for their help

GETTING READY TO SHARE

Making Meaning® Teacher

Some questions in this lesson are similar to those asked in *Making Meaning* Unit 8, Week 2, Days 3 and 4. Read the lessons in both programs and decide if you want to teach them separately or combine them into one experience for the students. It is not necessary to ask the same question in both lessons.

Teacher Note

Some ways students have helped each other to become better writers this year include: brainstorming ideas together, giving each other feedback, working on some writing projects together (such as the nonfiction informational piece), asking each other questions about their writing, and showing interest and appreciation when sharing from the Author's Chair.

1▶ Reflect on Classroom Writing Community

Have the students stay at their desks today. Remind them that they reflected on how they have grown as writers earlier in the week. Explain that today they will have a chance to think about how they did with becoming a safe and caring writing community this year and how they have personally grown as members of the community.

Have the students close their eyes and visualize as you ask each of the following questions. Pause between each question to give them time to think.

Q *What has it felt like to be a part of our writing community this year?*

Q *What have you done to contribute to our community this year?*

Q *What are three things your partners or classmates have done to help you become a better writer this year?*

Have the students open their eyes, turn to the next blank page in their writing notebooks, and write the three things their classmates or partners have done to help them become better writers this year

After the students have had time to list their ideas, signal for their attention.

SHARING AND REFLECTING

2 ### Share Reflections and Thank One Another

Gather the class in a circle and have them bring their writing notebooks. Explain that each student will choose one of the three things they listed to read aloud to the class. Point out that it is important to take time to thank people who have been helpful to them, and invite them to say "Thank you" to the class after reading their selection aloud.

Give the students a moment to select what they will read aloud. Then go around the room and have each student read his selection aloud, followed by "Thank you." When all the students have read their selections, ask and discuss:

Q *How have we done at creating a caring and safe community this year? What makes you think so?*

Q *How have you grown in your ability to work with partners this year?*

Students might say:

"I think we did a good job of becoming a community this year. Whenever we had problems, we talked about them so we could get along better."

"I agree with [Paulie], because the more we got to know each other, the more we were a community."

"I used to be too shy to talk to my partner, but now I feel I can talk to any partner I have."

You might want to share some of your general observations about ways your students have changed or grown as members of the community over the year.

Encourage the students to continue to write and to become caring members of their classroom writing community next year.

Teacher Note

You might say, "I remember how some students didn't want to work with their assigned partner at the beginning of the year. Now you are much better at working with any partner. I also notice that you relied much more heavily on me at the beginning of the year to help you solve your problems. Now you are able to solve many problems by yourself."

Writing Habits of Professional Authors

"Get up very early and get going at once; in fact [write] first and
wash afterwards."

— W. H. Auden

"I generally write for three or four hours at a sitting, mornings as
a rule."

— Saul Bellow

"The writer…withdraws to some quiet corner, a bedroom perhaps,
or any cubicle with a chair and a table, and applies himself to his
blank paper. Two hours a day are needed, three hours are better,
four are heroic."

— Gerald Warner Brace

"My goal is to write only one sentence a day. I write this on the bus
on my way to work. I usually find that I write more than just one
sentence, but the important point is that I have accomplished the
goal I set by 9:00 A.M."

— Lavinia Dobler

"I keep a typewriter with a sheet of paper in it on the end of the
kitchen table. When I have a five-minute lull and the children are
playing quietly, I sit down and knock out a paragraph."

— Lois Duncan

"I have a nice teak desk, long and wide, on which I keep special
things: crisp new legal pads and No. 2 pencils with good rubber
erasers that don't leave red smears; a dark blue draftsman lamp that
twists and bends like a tall, limber skeleton; a small quartz clock
that silently flicks the minutes…and an orange tomcat who lies on a
blanket and snores."

— Gail Godwin

Appendices

Grade 5 Skill Development Chart

X = skill taught (practiced)

Writing Process / Skill (code)	Publication	Proofreading	Revision	Drafting	Prewriting	Cite books and magazines	Capitalize proper nouns	Use single and double quotation marks in speech and direct quotations	Recognize and use conjunctions to connect ideas	Recognize and consistently use first- and third-person points of view	Recognize and consistently use past, present, and future verb tenses	Correctly use commonly misused words	Recognize and divide run-on and very long sentences	Recognize parts of speech
5.1.1				X	X									
5.1.2				X	X									
5.1.3				X	X									
5.1.4				X	X									
5.2.1			X											
5.2.2			X											X
5.2.3	X	X	X				X							
5.3.1				X	X									
5.3.2				X	X									
5.3.3			X											
5.3.4	X	X	X				X		X	X				
5.4.1				X	X									
5.4.2				X	X			X						
5.4.3				X	X									
5.4.4			X											
5.4.5				X	X					X				X
5.4.6	X	X	X				X	X	X	X			X	X
5.5.1					X									
5.5.2					X									
5.5.3				X	X									
5.5.4				X										
5.5.5			X											
5.5.6	X	X	X			X	X	X	X	X	X	X	X	
5.6.1				X	X									
5.6.2				X	X									
5.6.3	X	X	X			X	X	X	X	X	X	X	X	
5.7.1				X	X									
5.7.2				X	X									
5.7.3	X	X	X											
5.8.1	X			X	X									

Bibliography

Ainsworth, Mary. "Patterns of Attachment Behaviour Shown by the Infant in Interaction with His Mother." *Merrill-Palmer Quarterly* 10 (1964): 51–58.

Anderson, Richard C., and P. David Pearson. "A Schema-Theoretic View of Basic Process in Reading Comprehension." In *Handbook of Reading Research* edited by P. David Pearson. New York: Longman, 1984.

Asher, James J. "Children Learning Another Language: A Developmental Hypothesis." *Child Development* 48 (1977): 1040–48.

———. "Children's First Language as a Model for Second Language Learning." *Modern Language Journal* 56 (1972): 133–39.

———. "The Strategy of Total Physical Response: An Application to Learning Russian." *International Review of Applied Linguistics* 3 (1965): 291–300.

Atwell, Nancie. *In the Middle: New Understandings About Writing, Reading, and Learning.* Portsmouth, NH: Heinemann-Boynton/Cook, 1998.

Battistich, Victor, Daniel Solomon, Dong-il Kim, Marilyn Watson, and Eric Schaps. "Schools as Communities, Poverty Levels of Student Populations, and Students' Attitudes, Motives, and Performance: A Multilevel Analysis." *American Educational Research Journal* 32, no. 3 (Fall 1995): 627–58.

Beck, Isabel L., Margaret G. McKeown, and Linda Kucan. *Bringing Words to Life: Robust Vocabulary Instruction.* New York: Guilford Press, 2002.

Bowlby, John. *Attachment and Loss.* Vol 1, *Attachment.* New York: Basic Books, 1997.

Calkins, Lucy. *The Art of Teaching Writing.* Portsmouth, NH: Heinemann, 1994.

Contestable, Julie W., Shaila Regan, Susie Alldredge, Carol Westrich, and Laurel Robertson. *Number Power: A Cooperative Approach to Mathematics and Social Development Grades K–6.* Oakland, CA: Developmental Studies Center, 1999.

Culham, Ruth. *6+1 Traits of Writing: The Complete Guide for the Primary Grades.* Portland, OR: Northwest Regional Educational Laboratory, 2005.

———. *6+1 Traits of Writing: The Complete Guide, Grades 3 and Up.* Portland, OR: Northwest Regional Educational Laboratory, 2003.

Cummins, James. "The Role of Primary Language Development in Promoting Educational Success for Language Minority Students." In *Schooling and Language Minority Students: A Theoretical Framework*. Los Angeles: California State University, Evaluation, Dissemination, and Assessment Center, 1981.

Cunningham, Anne E., and Keith E. Stanovich. "What Reading Does for the Mind." *American Educator*, Spring/Summer 1998: 8–15.

Developmental Studies Center. *Blueprints for a Collaborative Classroom*. Oakland, CA: Developmental Studies Center, 1997.

———. *Ways We Want Our Class to Be*. Oakland, CA: Developmental Studies Center, 1996.

DeVries, Rheta, and Betty Zan. *Moral Classrooms, Moral Children*. New York: Teachers College Press, 1994.

Dewey, John. *Democracy and Education*. New York: Macmillan, 1916.

Fletcher, Ralph, and JoAnn Portalupi. *Writing Workshop: The Essential Guide*. Portsmouth, NH: Heinemann, 2001.

Flood, James, Dianne Lapp, and Julie M. Jensen. *The Handbook of Research on Teaching the English Language*. Mahwah, NJ: Lawrence Erlbaum Associates, 2002.

Freedman, Sarah W., Linda Flower, Glynda Hull, and J. R. Hayes. "Ten Years of Research: Achievements of the National Center for the Study of Writing and Literacy." In *A Handbook for Literacy Educators: Research on Teaching the Communicative and Visual Arts*, edited by J. Flood, S. B. Heath, and D. Lapp. Forthcoming.

Gambrell, Linda B., Lesley Mandel Morrow, Susan B. Neuman, and Michael Pressley, eds. *Best Practices in Literacy Instruction*. New York: Guilford Press, 1999.

Graves, Donald H. "Children Can Write Authentically If We Help Them." *Primary Voices K–6* 1, no. 1 (2003): 2–6.

Graves, Donald H. *Writing: Teachers and Children at Work*. Portsmouth, NH: Heinemann, 2003.

Hakuta, Kenji, Yuko Goto Butler, and Daria Witt. *How Long Does It Take English Learners to Attain Proficiency?* Santa Barbara, CA: University of California, Linguistic Minority Research Institute, 2000.

Harvey, Stephanie. *Nonfiction Matters: Reading, Writing, and Research in Grades 3–8*. York, ME: Stenhouse Publishers, 1998.

Herrell, Adrienne L. *Fifty Strategies for Teaching English Language Learners.* Upper Saddle River, NJ: Merrill, 2000.

Johnson, David W., Roger T. Johnson, and Edythe Johnson Holubec. *The New Circles of Learning: Cooperation in the Classroom.* Alexandria, VA: Association for Supervision and Curriculum Development, 1994.

Kagan, Spencer. *Cooperative Learning.* San Juan Capistrano, CA: Resources of Teachers, 1992.

Kamil, Michael L., Peter B. Mosenthal, P. David Pearson, and Rebecca Barr, eds. *Handbook of Reading Research, Volume III.* Mahwah, NJ: Lawrence Erlbaum Associates, 2000.

Kelley, Michael C. *Teachers' Reports of Writing Instruction at a High Performing Elementary School.* University of Delaware: Doctoral dissertation, 2002.

Kohlberg, Lawrence. *The Psychology of Moral Development.* New York: Harper and Row, 1984.

Kohn, Alfie. *Beyond Discipline: From Compliance to Community.* Alexandria, VA: Association for Supervision and Curriculum Development, 1996.

———. *Punished by Rewards: The Trouble with Gold Stars, Incentive Plans, A's, Praise, and Other Bribes.* New York: Houghton Mifflin Company, 1999.

Krashen, Stephen D. *Principles and Practice in Second Language Acquisition.* New York: Prentice-Hall, 1982.

———. *Second Language Acquisition and Second Language Learning.* New York: Pergamon Press, 1981.

———. "TPR: Still a Very Good Idea." *NovELTy* 5, no. 4 (1998).

———, and Tracy D. Terrell. *The Natural Approach: Language Acquisition in the Classroom.* Englewood Cliffs, NJ: Prentice Hall, 1983.

National Commission on Writing in America's Colleges and Schools. *The Neglected "R": The Need for a Writing Revolution.* New York: College Board, 2003.

National Council of Teachers of English. *What We Know About Writing: Early Literacy.* NCTE Writing Initiative. www.ncte.org/prog/writing/research/113328.htm.

National Governor's Association for Best Practices. *Making Writing Instruction Work.* Washington, DC: National Governor's Association Center for Best Practices, 2001.

Nucci, Larry P., ed. *Moral Development and Character Education: A Dialogue.* Berkeley, CA: McCutchan Publishing Corporation, 1989.

Optiz, Michael F., ed. *Literacy Instruction for Culturally and Linguistically Diverse Students.* Newark, DE: International Reading Association, 1998.

Piaget, Jean. *The Child's Conception of the World.* Trans. Joan and Andrew Tomlinson. Lanham, MD: Littlefield Adams, 1969.

———. *The Moral Judgment of the Child.* Trans. Marjorie Gabain. New York: The Free Press, 1965.

Ray, Katie Wood. *About the Authors: Writing Workshop with Our Youngest Writers.* Portsmouth, NH: Heinemann, 2004.

Resnick, Michael D., P. S. Bearman, R. W. Blum, K. E. Bauman, K. M. Harris, J. Jones, J. Tabor, et al. "Protecting Adolescents from Harm: Findings from the National Longitudinal Study on Adolescent Health." *Journal of the American Medical Association* 278 (1997): 823–32.

Schaps, Eric, Victor Battistich, and Dan Solomon. "Community in School a Key to Student Growth: Findings from the Child Development Project." In *Building School Success on Social and Emotional Learning,* edited by R. Weissberg, J. Zins, and H. Walbert. New York: Teachers College Press, 2004.

Schaps, Eric, Catherine Lewis, and Marilyn Watson. "Building Classroom Communities." *Thrust for Educational Leadership,* September 1997.

Schaps, Eric, Esther F. Schaeffer, and Sanford N. McDonnell. "What's Right and Wrong in Character Education Today." *Education Week,* September 12, 2001: 40–44.

Shefelbine, John, and Katherine K. Newman. *SIPPS: Systematic Instruction in Phoneme Awareness, Phonics, and Sight Words.* Oakland, CA: Developmental Studies Center, 2005.

Sulzby, Elizabeth. "Research Directions: Transitions from Emergent to Conventional Writing." *Language Arts* 69 (1992): 290–97.

Swain, M., and S. Lapkin. "Problems in Output and the Cognitive Processes They Generate: A Step Toward Second Language Learning." *Applied Linguistics* 16, no. 3 (1995): 371–91.

William, Joan A. "Classroom Conversations: Opportunities to Learn for ESL Students in Mainstream Classrooms." *The Reading Teacher* 54, no. 8 (2001): 750–57.

Blackline Masters

Excerpts

Passages About Sharks (1)

Great whites do some strange things **while** they are hunting. They have been seen poking their heads out of the water, **perhaps** to look around for seals sunning themselves on rocks.

Recently scientists have seen what fishermen have been telling them for years: great white sharks can leap nearly out of the water to pursue their prey. Off the coasts of California and South Africa, researchers have photographed great whites jumping straight out of the water. **Usually** the sharks were attacking their natural prey—seals or sea lions that may leap out of the water themselves to escape their enemies. **Other times** the sharks were chasing plastic decoys that researchers towed behind their boats.

— from *The Truth About Great White Sharks*

- - - - - - - - - - - - -

continues

Excerpts from *The Truth About Great White Sharks* © 2000 by Mary M. Cerullo (text); Jeffrey L. Rottman (photographs). Used with permission of Chronicle Books LLC, San Francisco. Visit chroniclebooks.com.

Great whites visit the coasts of northern California, South Africa, and southern Australia **when** seals, sea lions, and elephant seals come onto land to give birth.

Great whites roam the cool waters of the world's oceans **but** they aren't common anywhere. **Although** great whites will come together to feed on the same prey, they usually don't travel in schools or even in pairs.

— from *The Truth About Great White Sharks*

Excerpts from *The Truth About Great White Sharks* © 2000 by Mary M. Cerullo (text); Jeffrey L. Rottman (photographs). Used with permission of Chronicle Books LLC, San Francisco. Visit chroniclebooks.com.

Unpunctuated Nonfiction Paragraph

A raging wildfire is a frightening thing living trees burn as fast as cardboard boxes in a bonfire flames race through the treetops sometimes faster than a person can run burning at temperatures hot enough to melt steel a wildfire can be a major disaster capable of destroying hundreds of homes and costing human lives.

— from *Wildfires*

Excerpts from *Wildfires* © 1996 by Seymour Simon used by permission of HarperCollins Publishers.

Essay

School Uniforms
by Akinyi R., Westford, MA
adapted from www.teenink.com

Are school uniforms appropriate for public school students? Yes, and I believe students in public school should be required to wear them. Uniforms eliminate the distractions of designer clothes so students can focus on their studies. Uniforms also create an environment in which children will be judged on personality rather than style. Finally, uniforms save time and money.

While attending a parochial school, I experienced the luxury of wearing uniforms. At my school, students came from diverse backgrounds. Inside the building, however, our economic advantages or disadvantages were no longer obvious. My friends and I were able to focus on academics and concern for others rather than the latest fashions. Since we looked similar, we remained attentive to the teacher and our work. I learned that my effort, attitude and aptitude were more important than my clothes.

Wearing uniforms helped me realize I don't need to impress anyone by the clothes I wear. School uniforms

continues

helped children who did not have "stylish" clothes to be treated fairly. I was judged by my character, not the price of my jeans. I had a chance to show my personality without worry that I was out of style. This set the tone in the school system that all individuals were to be treated as equals.

I never had to waste time deciding what to wear before school. A clean uniform was easy to maintain. My parents saved a lot of money, too. I did not need a variety of colors, styles and designer fashions in my wardrobe. Wearing uniforms helped me learn I did not always have to buy clothes I wanted when I wanted them.

When I wore a uniform, I started my day worry-free, focused on my schoolwork and felt judged by who I was on the inside. My family and I saved time and money. I believe children should be required to wear uniforms in public schools.

"School Uniforms" reprinted by permission of Teen Ink magazine and TeenInk.com

Essay

WARNING: Too Much TV Is Hazardous to Your Health
adapted from www.tvturnoff.org

More than four hours a day: that's how much television Americans watch on average. As an abundance of evidence makes clear, our television habit has serious negative consequences. Excessive TV-watching cuts into family time, harms our kids' ability to read and perform well in school, encourages violence, and promotes sedentary lifestyles and obesity.

TV Undermines Family Time

Many people feel that they do not have enough time to spend with their families...television plays a crucial role. In the average American household, the TV is on for 7 hours, 40 minutes a day, and 40 percent of Americans report always or often watching television while eating dinner. Families who watch little or no television often find that they have more time to spend with one another.

TV Harms Reading and Academic Performance

Excessive television-watching harms reading skills... researcher[s] [found] more than a decade ago that "reading scores diminished sharply for those students watching

continues

more than four hours a day." Researchers such as Jane Healy of Harvard argue that watching TV instead of reading may actually [change] the physical structure of the brain as it develops, making learning and working in the schoolroom environment difficult.

TV Encourages Violence

The evidence is overwhelming: violence on TV promotes violent behavior in real life. Of more than 3,500 research studies on the effects of media violence over the past 40 years, 99.5 percent have shown a positive correlation between watching violence on TV and committing acts of real-life violence.

TV Promotes Sedentary Lifestyles and Obesity

Americans, by and large, do not get enough physical exercise. We spend most of our free time watching television, which promotes obesity and its related illnesses. According to Dr. William Dietz at the Centers for Disease Control, "The easiest way to reduce inactivity is to turn off the TV set. Almost anything else uses more energy than watching TV."

Essay

Television: The Most Disparaged Resource of the Information Age

by Salmaan S., Westford, MA

adapted from www.teenink.com

Almost every day one can hear some mention of "The TV generation of the '90s." Many harshly label television as a "drug," claiming that millions of children every day waste their time in front of this electronic altar. Well, I strongly disagree with the viewpoint that television is a waste of time.

Today, there are many different ways to transfer thoughts and ideas. Of these, television, with its combination of audio-visual stimuli, is one of the quickest to present an idea clearly and completely. To say that television is not important is to say that learning about other cultures thousands of miles away by seeing and hearing is a waste of time. In this age of information, television is one of the most efficient means of mass communication available to man.

continues

Where else could billions of people have [seen] the horrors of the Tiananmen Square incident or witnessed firsthand man's first steps on the moon? In what other way could people have simultaneously experienced the fall of the Berlin Wall or Vietnam?

Television unites mankind because people separated by distance, skin color, language and wealth can all relate to some of the things they see on TV. No other appliance of the information age is as quick and widely used around the world as television. Failing to acknowledge the positive value of this resource to mankind is an enormous mistake.

"Television: The Most Disparaged Resource of the Information Age" reprinted by permission of Teen Ink magazine and TeenInk.com.

Unpunctuated Passage from a Persuasive Essay (1)

Louis Pasteur a french chemist helped save animals as well as humans when he developed a vaccine for rabies using animal experimentation today animal lovers everywhere do not have to put their pets to sleep if they get rabies instead they can just go to their veterinarian and get this preventive vaccine

nobody I know of in biological research who has to sacrifice animals likes it says Richard Jones a biology professor at colorado university it is a matter of priorities you work for the greater good.

— from "Animal Experimentation Saves Lives"

"Animal Experimentation Saves Lives" reprinted by permission of Teen Ink magazine and TeenInk.com.

Unpunctuated Passage from a Persuasive Essay (2)

TV promotes sedentary lifestyles and obesity

Americans by and large do not get enough physical exercise we spend most of our free time watching television which promotes obesity and its related illnesses according to Dr William Dietz at the centers for disease control the easiest way to reduce inactivity is to turn off the TV set almost anything else uses more energy than watching TV.

> — from "WARNING: Too Much TV
> Is Hazardous to Your Health"

Poetry

Child Frightened by a Thunderstorm
by Ted Kooser

Thunder has nested in the grass all night
and rumpled it, and with its outstretched wings
has crushed the peonies. Its beak was bright,
sharper than garden shears and, clattering,
it snipped its bouquets of branches for its bed.
I could not sleep. The thunder's eyes were red.

flamingo
by Valerie Worth

The
Flamingo
Lingers
A
Long
Time
Over
One
Pink
Leg;

Later
He
Ponders
Upon
The
Other
For
A
While
Instead.

"flamingo" from *All the Small Poems and Fourteen More* by Valerie Worth, pictures by Natalie Babbitt. Copyright © 1987, 1994 by Valerie Worth. Reprinted by permission of Farrar, Straus and Giroux, LLC.

Poetry

Windshield Wiper
by Eve Merriam

fog smog	fog smog
tissue paper	tissue paper
clear the blear	clear the smear
fog more	fog more
splat splat	downpour
rubber scraper	rubber scraper
overshoes	macintosh
bumbershoot	muddle on
slosh through	slosh through
drying up	drying up
sky lighter	sky lighter
nearly clear	nearly clear
clearing	clearing veer
clear here	clear

I Love the Look of Words
by Maya Angelou

Popcorn leaps, popping from the floor
of a hot black skillet
and into my mouth.
Black words leap
snapping from the white
page. Rushing into my eyes. Sliding
into my brain which gobbles them
the way my tongue and teeth
chomp the buttered popcorn.

When I have stopped reading,
ideas from the words stay stuck
in my mind, like the sweet
smell of butter perfuming my
fingers long after the popcorn
is finished.

I love the book and the look of words
the weight of ideas that popped into my mind
I love the tracks
of new thinking in my mind.

Being a Writer Reorder Information

Grade 3

Additional Units

Poetry Genre Unit (Teacher's Manual and CD-ROM Reproducible Materials)	BWA-GU3-1
Letter Writing Genre Unit (Teacher's Manual, 2 trade books, and CD-ROM Reproducible Materials)	BWA-GU3-2
Additional Genre Units Package (Poetry Genre Unit and Letter Writing Genre Unit)	BWA-GUP3-1
Preparing for a Writing Test, Grades 3–5 (Teacher's Manual and CD-ROM Reproducible Materials)	BWA-PWT35

Classroom Package — BW-CP3

Contents: Teacher's Manual (2 volumes), Skill Practice Teaching Guide, Assessment Resource Book, 25 Student Writing Handbooks, 25 Student Skill Practice Books, and 33 trade books.

Available separately

Teacher's Manual, vol. 1	BW-TM3-V1
Teacher's Manual, vol. 2	BW-TM3-V2
Skill Practice Teaching Guide	BW-STG3
Assessment Resource Book	BW-AB3
Student Writing Handbook pack (5 books)	BW-SB3-Q5
Student Skill Practice Book pack (5 books)	BW-SSB3-Q5
CD-ROM Grade 3 Reproducible Materials	BW-CDR3
Trade book set (33 books)	BW-TBS3

Grade 4

Additional Units

Persuasive Nonfiction Genre Unit (Teacher's Manual and CD-ROM Reproducible Materials)	BWA-GU4-1
Letter Writing Genre Unit (Teacher's Manual and CD-ROM Reproducible Materials)	BWA-GU4-2
Additional Genre Units Package (Persuasive Nonfiction Genre Unit and Letter Writing Genre Unit)	BWA-GUP4-1
Preparing for a Writing Test, Grades 3–5 (Teacher's Manual and CD-ROM Reproducible Materials)	BWA-PWT35

Classroom Package — BW-CP4

Contents: Teacher's Manual (2 volumes), Skill Practice Teaching Guide, Assessment Resource Book, 30 Student Writing Handbooks, 30 Student Skill Practice Books, and 25 trade books.

Available separately

Teacher's Manual, vol. 1	BW-TM4-V1
Teacher's Manual, vol. 2	BW-TM4-V2
Skill Practice Teaching Guide	BW-STG4
Assessment Resource Book	BW-AB4
Student Writing Handbook pack (5 books)	BW-SB4-Q5
Student Skill Practice Book pack (5 books)	BW-SSB4-Q5
CD-ROM Grade 4 Reproducible Materials	BW-CDR4
Trade book set (25 books)	BW-TBS4

Grade 5

Additional Units

Letter Writing Genre Unit (Teacher's Manual, 1 trade book, and CD-ROM Reproducible Materials)	BWA-GU5-1
Functional Writing Genre Unit (Teacher's Manual and CD-ROM Reproducible Materials)	BWA-GU5-2
Additional Genre Units Package (Letter Writing Genre Unit and Functional Writing Genre Unit)	BWA-GUP5-1
Preparing for a Writing Test, Grades 3–5 (Teacher's Manual and CD-ROM Reproducible Materials)	BWA-PWT35

Classroom Package — BW-CP5

Contents: Teacher's Manual (2 volumes), Skill Practice Teaching Guide, Assessment Resource Book, 30 Student Writing Handbooks, 30 Student Skill Practice Books, and 25 trade books.

Available separately

Teacher's Manual, vol. 1	BW-TM5-V1
Teacher's Manual, vol. 2	BW-TM5-V2
Skill Practice Teaching Guide	BW-STG5
Assessment Resource Book	BW-AB5
Student Writing Handbook pack (5 books)	BW-SB5-Q5
Student Skill Practice Book pack (5 books)	BW-SSB5-Q5
CD-ROM Grade 5 Reproducible Materials	BW-CDR5
Trade book set (25 books)	BW-TBS5

Grade 6

Additional Units

Letter Writing Genre Unit (Teacher's Manual, 1 trade book, and CD-ROM Reproducible Materials)	BWA-GU6-1
Functional Writing Genre Unit (Teacher's Manual, 1 trade book, and CD-ROM Reproducible Materials)	BWA-GU6-2
Additional Genre Units Package (Letter Writing Genre Unit and Functional Writing Genre Unit)	BWA-GUP6-1

Classroom Package — BW-CP6

Contents: Teacher's Manual (2 volumes), Skill Practice Teaching Guide, Assessment Resource Book, 30 Student Writing Handbooks (2 volumes), 30 Student Skill Practice Books, and 14 trade books.

Available separately

Teacher's Manual, vol. 1	BW-TM6-V1
Teacher's Manual, vol. 2	BW-TM6-V2
Skill Practice Teaching Guide	BW-STG6
Assessment Resource Book	BW-AB6
Student Writing Handbook pack (5 books)	BW-SB6-Q5
Student Skill Practice Book pack (5 books)	BW-SSB6-Q5
CD-ROM Grade 6 Reproducible Materials	BW-CDR6
Trade book set (14 books)	BW-TBS6

The *Being a Writer* program is also available at grades K–2. Visit www.devstu.org for more information.

Ordering Information:

To order call 800.666.7270 * fax 510.842.0348 * log on to www.devstu.org * e-mail pubs@devstu.org

Or Mail Your Order to:

Developmental Studies Center * Publications Department * 2000 Embarcadero, Suite 305 * Oakland, CA 94606-530

DEVELOPMENTAL STUDIES CENTER